The Remarkable Kyles
by Denis O'Hara

To Janine

& Thank you for your
support for the sport !

we love

Maeve & Ge...

ISBN 10: 0-9554719-0-7

ISBN 13: 078-0-95547-19-0-2

Published by O'Hara Publications,
Martinstown Co. Antrim NI.

Designed by Print Promotions,
Ballymena Co. Antrim NI.

Printed by W&G Baird Ltd.
Greystone Press. Antrim Co. Antrim NI.

Photographs in this publication are mainly from the Kyle Collection.
Also by kind permission of the News Letter, Belfast Telegraph, Irish News,
Press Association, Sunday Life, Irish Independent, Sunday Independent, Irish
Times, Fairplay Magazine, Ballymena Guardian, Antrim Guardian, Ballymena
Times, Coaching Northern Ireland, and the University of Ulster Jordanstown.

Copyright holders of some photographs could not be established, despite a
widespread search. We apologise if, by being unable to trace other photograph
source, we have failed to acknowledge copyright material.

Acknowledgments
to the
Editorial Team
With Grateful Thanks

Editor - Paul Welsh

Catherine O'Hara

Orla WIlkinson

Mairead Magill

Elizabeth O'Hara

Barbara McCartney

Kathleen McGowan

Tim Wallace

Contents

FOREWORD
by Ronnie Delany

It is a delight to be associated with this appreciation, including the celebration of Maeve Kyle's life and career, over 50 years of marriage to Sean, and her association with the Ballymena and Antrim Athletics Club - also for over 50 years.

We were Olympians - and once an Olympian, always an Olympian. Maeve and I shared this unique first adventure in 1956, when we both took part in the Melbourne Games.

It was a much different experience in those days than today. Travel was arduous and lengthy, crossing the Pacific. Also, the lack of backup for athletes was totally different. We had no team manager for athletics. We had no doctors. What we had was each other - and that was important.

My memories of Maeve go back to pre-Melbourne. I have a very lengthy relationship with Maeve's family, back to when I was a novice athlete. I happened to be working in Kilkenny, where I had the privilege of using the track facility at the College, where Maeve's father was the headmaster.

Her younger brother, Brian Shankey was a very good 200 metres runner. My own brother Joe was also involved. He was a superb athlete, winning boys and men's races at the same time. He ran 200 metres, and was also a good jumper - with an incredible spring. He could jump almost 22 feet 10 inches on grass!

The reason I was in Kilkenny was through a career decision. I went to work there, in a job as a salesman - but I had ambitions to be an athlete. I felt I could accomplish that by leaving my home, and going down to Kilkenny. The selling job gave me a chance to train during the day.

My brother Joe would have known Maeve. I did not, at that very early stage of my career. Maeve would have been married to Sean by then. Later on, I got to know Sean, and was often invited to their home. They are an incredible couple.

I also met some of the Ballymena Club's athletes, such as Lorna McGarvey, in the company of Maeve and Sean at their lovely home in Ballymena. No one ever had a more appropriate house name than that of Tir-na-nOg (meaning Land of the Young).

I consider myself very fortunate to be able to call her my friend for all those years - and, indeed, Sean, her husband. I also got to know their daughter Shauna.

So, we go back a long time. I admire Maeve greatly, because of her contribution to sport in close on six decades! Her own achievements are well chronicled, but what isn't known is the enormous respect people like me hold for Maeve Kyle... and how we appreciate her in person to this very day.

For example, when the relay teams were taking part in Sydney 2000, where she had a management role, her influence was apparent on the quality of baton changing - and, indeed, on the achievements of the team.

On a personal level, I send her my love, and on a professional level - what a wonderful contribution she made to sport over the years. Maeve and Sean deserve the many accolades. I say well done.

I left my university, Villanova, in early November 1956 to go to the Olympics, and after we left Melbourne - before the tournament ended, I went straight back to university in Philadelphia.

The rest of the team members went on to Ireland, where they were extremely well received. On the way down to the Melbourne Olympics, I joined the Ireland team in New York. We went to San Francisco, and stayed there for a week. I enjoyed the training in California.

There were different experiences, and you created close friendships out of these experiences. That was the thing with sports people. There was enormous close bonding.

The number of friends Maeve developed over the years in the Olympic movement is incredible! She was an elite sports person at so many Olympics. Maeve was also an elite hockey player, so she has an immense range of friends. All of whom, including people like myself, have the greatest respect and affection for her. You may get a few odd cribs about her. There is no one who gets away scot-free.

We keep close contact. We shared things together. We were on the Sports Council together, for years. I have also been a member of the Lifeboats Committee since 1972, and visited Cushendall and Red Bay many times in the past - so, when I'm on a trip to the Glens of Antrim I also call in to see the remarkable Kyles.

COMMENDATION
Mayor of Ballymena

We are honoured and proud to have sporting legends Maeve and Sean Kyle represented on our Hall of Fame at Ballymena Showgrounds. They sit alongside other Borough sporting greats such as Dr. Sydney Millar, Mary Peters DBE and Willie John Mc Bride. Their presence here portrays a lifetime of sporting achievements in athletics and coaching second to none.

They have both achieved phenomenal sporting success and continue to contribute to the sporting life of the Borough through their dedicated involvement in Ballymena and Antrim Athletic Club. The club, founded by Sean Kyle in 1954 is one of the top track and fields club in the country. Even though Maeve and Sean are both in their seventies, they still adopt a hands on approach in nurturing young local talent through the club.

Maeve continues to motivate all those she comes in contact with and together with Sean has been responsible for bringing the British and Irish Veterans International Cross Country Championships to Ballymena every few years. This is easily among some of the biggest sporting events to come to Ballymena ever. Their involvement with this event has allowed large numbers of participants and visitors from England, Ireland, Scotland and Wales to visit the town of Ballymena to enjoy what we have to offer.

Through sport Maeve and Sean have brought communities together and through sport they have given the world a positive image of Ballymena, and I thank them for that.

Alderman James Alexander

Mayor of Ballymena

APPRECIATION
by Pat Hickey

It is a delightful fact one of the great partnerships in Irish sport for decades has been that of Maeve and Sean Kyle – a partnership that has yielded immense benefits to hundreds of athletes, North and South, as well as having a very important Olympic dimension.

It's been all about performance, commitment, exceptional coaching, constant striving for excellence, and for sporting success – a perfect partnership with a personal touch, one that continues to awaken the imagination of athletes and sports fans throughout Ireland, and beyond.

Maeve has graced the Olympic stage in Melbourne, Rome and Tokyo and performed a vital coaching role for the Irish athletics squad at the Sydney Olympics. Maeve and Sean have coached scores of athletes for other top events such as World and European championships, the Commonwealth Games, and many Olympic qualifiers.

Their guidance, expertise and continuing influence has been widespread - and has paid many important dividends off the track as well as on it. The cross community support that their home club, Ballymena & Antrim A.C., has enjoyed through difficult times in the North is as great a legacy to Maeve and Sean, as is their many outstanding athletic achievements.

On behalf of the Olympic Movement, let me fully endorse this publication. For over 50 years, the dynamic pairing of Maeve and Sean has served their club, their community and Irish sport magnificently - and long may they continue to motivate and inspire us with their work.

In this book their enthralling life story is told for the first time, and told well. Enjoy!

PAT HICKEY
President of the European Olympic Committee
President of the Olympic Council of Ireland
Irish member of the International Olympic Committee.

8

**Message
from Professor Eric Saunders, OBE.**

Chairman, Sports Council for Northern Ireland

"**We** are delighted to be associated with the publication about "The Remarkable Kyles." This book is dedicated to two athletes who have committed their lives to sport. Many would say it was fate that brought Maeve and Sean together, consequently their partnership had enormous effects on athletics in Northern Ireland.

Training and coaching young people in Ballymena and Antrim Athletics Club have enabled young athletes to reach national and world class status, such as the talented Anna Boyle.

One of the key aims of the strategy for the Sports Council for Northern Ireland is concerned with helping athletes strive for excellence. Maeve and Sean are key examples of coaches who enable athletes reach their optimum level of achievement in their desired sport."

**Eric Saunders, OBE
Chairman, Sports Council for Northern Ireland**

SPORTS
COUNCIL NORTHERN IRELAND

9

COMMENDATION

The Mayor of Antrim

For the past 52 years, Ballymena & Antrim Athletics Club has a well-deserved reputation for producing champions through the high level of coaching provided by some of the most revered coaches in Ireland. Had it not been for the drive and dedication of two remarkable people, Maeve and Sean Kyle this might not have been the case.

From a personal point of view, I had the opportunity to become well acquainted with Maeve and Sean through the Antrim Sports Advisory Association (ASAA), and I have found their input to the ASAA invaluable.

Antrim Stadium is one of only three international tracks in Northern Ireland and I am delighted that Maeve and Sean chose Antrim as the home of the Ballymena & Antrim Athletics Club. Many of their 'trainees', too numerous to mention, have been selected for the UK Championships, the Commonwealth Games and the ultimate accolade, the Olympics Games.

Indeed, this husband and wife team have been such an inspiration, many of their athletes have gone on to break world records. Over the years, I have watched these athletes competing, knowing that if it hadn't been for Maeve and Sean, they wouldn't be where they are today.

In the course of their careers, the Kyles have received many awards in recognition of their coaching ability. However, this is the ultimate accolade - a book dedicated to them, and their love of sport.

I'm delighted to have had the opportunity to commend Maeve and Sean in such a lasting tribute, and I hope to watch many more of their achievements in the coming years.

Alderman Sam Dunlop

Mayor of Antrim

10

TRIBUTE
Coaching Northern Ireland

Maeve Kyle is one of those people I'm sure was placed on this planet to make a difference in people's lives. Maeve is an honest, straightforward, no-nonsense, inspiring coach, boss, mentor, granny, and a pillar of her community. Maeve Kyle is an astute business woman, an excellent coach and an accomplished Athlete.

I first met Maeve when I applied for the post of CEO of Coaching NI back in May 2003. At the interview, her questions were clear and to the point. She smiled, and made me feel at ease. I respected her immediately. Most people who meet Maeve Kyle feel the same way. During the past three and a half years my respect for Maeve and her husband Sean has grown considerably. My team members at Coaching NI have expressed similar sentiments.

Maeve is not only my boss she is a great friend and mentor. She never ceases to amaze me with her boundless energy and enthusiasm for sport, coaching and the business of leading the Board at Coaching NI. Maeve is also the right person to have beside you in a crisis, and can be assertive when necessary. In all her dealings with people Maeve acts with openness, integrity and honesty.

Maeve is a great public speaker, and almost always speaks without notes such is her knowledge and experience in the subjects of sport and coaching, whether it's speaking to coaches at the annual Coach of the Year Awards, to her peers at an International conference, or to the media, Maeve is at ease and very professional. Recently, I was in the audience as Maeve gave her acceptance speech for her Honorary Doctorate from the University of Ulster, at the Waterfront Hall, Belfast. In front of hundreds of graduates, Maeve spoke from the heart with no notes as if she was speaking to each individual person in the room - and asked them to say "thank you" to their school teachers, their University lecturers, parents and coaches. "Just say - thank you" was her message, and just the right message for such an occasion. It was indeed fitting Maeve was photographed on the day alongside a new graduate and one of Maeve's athletes, Anna Boyle.

No one really knows where life will lead us, but on the journey we will meet many people. I am glad I met Maeve Kyle.

Thank you Maeve.

Jim Gourley

CEO

Coaching NI

11

NOT ON FRIDAYS!

What a strange introduction to any book...never mind a book with a sporting theme. We hope you will understand the heading relates to essential private space during our coaching careers, indeed we should have added "or September". Though this is time free from practical coaching, it is the month of reflection, relaxation, refreshment and planning for next year's programme.

We have always worked as a team, initially with Sean, the coach, and Maeve, the athlete - and then Maeve learning to be a coach...from Sean.

This partnership developed into a solid working relationship, with Sean the ever-learning reader and researcher; Maeve the talent spotter and motivator.

We have bounced ideas, problems, plans and athlete responses off each other, usually finding a way forward with a joint decision. It has also been useful to have two pairs of eyes, to assess movement and technical details of athletes.

On a personal level, we have always been very close in thought and emotion, usually finishing each others sentences, or when apart ringing each other at the same time. This closeness has seen us through some tough times usually caused by external factors of misunderstanding or misinformation.

We have taken two steps backwards within our wider family of the Ballymena and Antrim Athletic Club, where we have so many "children" and "grandchildren", acquired over the years through our shared love of sport ... where we have been privileged to be part of so many lives and maybe to have added a little self belief or an understanding that rules, teamwork and helping each other is important in achieving results at every level.

Now, we are mentoring several of our retired international athletes, who are young, enthusiastic and who have been there - and who, we believe, will provide a seamless transition from now to then to ensure the club continues to lead the way in structure, development and achievement at every possible level.

We have seen an athlete who started her career in the club, and won Olympic gold, in Mary Peters; an athlete who spent her whole career in the club and won Commonwealth silver in Sharon McPeake - and athletes who rewrote the record books in middle distance running in Sean O'Neill, Mark Kirk and James McIlroy; hurdlers in C J Kirkpatrick and Elaine McLaughlin, long jumpers in Mark Forsythe and Billy Kirkpatrick, sprinters in Johnny Kilpatrick, Joe Chivers, Lorna and Noleen McGarvey, Simon Baird, Philip Snoddy and Johnny McAdorey, javelin in Ben Haughton, Michael Allen and Biddy Robinson, all-rounder throwers in Gay Porter, multi-eventers in Ray Knox and Mary Peters, and current stars such as Anna Boyle, Paul Brizzell, Gary Coulter, Leslie Leung, and many more ...... all some time club members.

These are some of the stars of past, present and future - but we are certain of our club record of always having athletes in the Northern Ireland Commonwealth team will continue, and with representation at all levels in both Ireland and the UK, the club will continue to be an ambassador for both Ballymena and Antrim and the wider territories it represents.

We will continue to be part of, and to help, the work of this great family that our club is part of, but not on Fridays - our personal time, and maybe not in September. -

Sean and Maeve Kyle

13

DEDICATION
Shauna Kyle - Daugther

As a child, life at home was pretty normal, just the usual routine of school homework and family life. Mum's training schedule was the centre of the routine. She even trained on Christmas Day, but once the session was over life at home was much like any other family.

Mum taught in Cambridge House School, where I was a pupil from the age of nine. She collected me from school at the end of each day. After training, mum made supper. I did my homework, and dad read his paper - and sometimes some of the other athletes stayed for supper too. At weekends in the winter, mum played hockey and did her winter training, so sometimes we went to Portstewart so she could train in the sand dunes - and I went off to explore on my own.

Sometimes, at weekends, mum was away either playing hockey or running. When I was little, I was sent to stay with my beloved Florence, who looked after me from the age of two. She lived in Portglenone, and mum used to put me on the bus which was scary but exciting too! Florence took me paddling, to the visiting funfair, and to the cinema. When I was a bit older, I used to stay at home with dad but, to be honest, his cooking was a bit of a disaster! Dad's "rubbery" cheese on toast is legend in the family.

Mum always made special occasions, like birthdays and Christmas, really special. We never open presents before the "big day" - and we do all the traditional things like stockings, and candles on cakes, and games on Christmas Night when friends call in.

One of the outstanding memories of my childhood is the fantasy cakes mum used to bake for my party every year. I once even had Cinderella's coach complete with white mice as the horses. How she did it I'll never know! She still bakes all the Christmas cakes and puddings for the family, and my daughter Indy helps her now . . . so the tradition carries on. We still have a sit-down family meal every Sunday, and Fridays have always been off limits to sport and are family-only days.

Holidays usually involved athletics, so we went to wherever mum was running for the meet, and then snatched a couple of days afterwards. This meant, as an only child, I was lucky enough to see most of Europe before I was 12. I vividly remember crossing Europe by train to the former Yugoslavia in 1962, when I slept in the luggage rack. Now we still sometimes go to major meets as a family, and Indy comes too. She went to the European Championships in Budapest, and had her face painted in team colours!

Most of all the values instilled into me by my parents, which I try to pass on to my daughter, have shaped me as a person. I was brought up to be honest, considerate of other people's feelings, loyal and most of all to be true to myself. It doesn't necessarily make life easy, especially in today's world, to stand up for what you believe is right, to stand up to bullies, to try to defend those less fortunate than yourself; to honour your promises and commitments - and to work as a team for the benefit of everyone not just yourself.

Those are the rules my parents have lived by, and passed on to me. I hope my daughter Indy is learning that it isn't always the easy path that rewards your spirit, but the courage of your convictions to stand up for what is right that counts.

Shauna Kyle

Introducing Icons

Four special tribute plaques that hang on the corridor wall leading to the Des Allen Suite, in the main Stand at Ballymena Showgrounds, encapsulate the sporting achievements of two outstanding track and field athletes, Maeve Kyle and Mary Peters, and two sons of the local soil, athletics coach Sean Kyle and rugby icon Syd Miller.

It is fitting the husband and wife combination of Sean and Maeve Kyle should be honoured in this way, not only for their respective achievements in athletics, and the 50th anniversary of their combined enterprising launch of the Ballymena Athletics club, but also the Golden Jubilee of their marriage.

The individual plaques are almost a floor-to-ceiling appreciation of the Kyle family's distinctive contribution to athletics. The potted history of Sean Kyle is perhaps more poignant than those of the other three recipients of All Star recognition. He spent a good part of his early life working in the interests of Ballymena Showgrounds, through the County Antrim Agricultural Association.

Chart notes declare . . ."Through his early commitment to the sport, and his instinctive and patient coaching, Sean laid the groundwork for Northern Ireland athletics. In 1954, Sean married Maeve, and the following year, on the basis of the local coaching he was already involved in, he founded the Ballymena and Antrim Athletics Club.

16

Mary Peters was one of the six founding athletes, and Sean would coach her for the first few years of her career. Sean remained Maeve's coach throughout, while he also coached many more local and international athletes. Sharon McPeake and Elizabeth McWilliams are just two of the athletes who have benefited from Sean's coaching over the years.

Throughout his coaching career there were a number of highlights for Sean. For twenty years he was the National Coach for Northern Ireland, and he also became the first Irish coach to be elected to the Association of World Coaches. In 1974, Sean was also presented with the Torch Trophy, the UK-wide recognition of voluntary work in sport.

Perhaps the ultimate accolade came from his peers, when he was named 'UK Coach of the Year' in 1987, with more than 40 years experience. Like the best runners, he has paced his career well; today he remains the Irish 800 metres and 1500 metres coach, after 60 years trackside, and he has acted as a senior official and is also a UK Master Coach.

Ballymena pays tribute to Sean for dedicating more than a lifetime to developing athletics in his hometown, and nurturing the sporting potential in people."

Side by side is the accolade to Maeve, who reveals: "I was the athlete, he was the coach."

This was the working ingredient to what developed quickly into one of the outstanding double acts in the history of athletics.

The main text declares: "Of course, before they met, Maeve was not even an athlete but had been a hockey international from the age of 19. Sean suggested athletics as a training method, accelerating her sporting career into a whirlwind of international track and field achievements; but her first commitment from start to finish has always been her hometown.

Maeve and Sean were married in 1954, and the following year they founded the Ballymena and Antrim Athletics Club. In 1956, at the age of 28, Maeve was selected for Ireland's Olympic team in the 100 and 200 metres, in spite of widespread lack of support for women's participation. Arrangements were very different from modern day Olympics, in that Maeve had to raise her own sponsorship to finance her trip, and when the solitary team official took ill Maeve had to step in as "mother" and arrange her team-mates' ironing and sewing.

For 14 years, Maeve competed at every international level - including three Olympics, two Commonwealth Games, two European Championships and the European Indoor Championships. In the 400 metres she set a new British record in 1961, becoming British champion and setting an indoor world record. She has

17

held more than fifty athletics titles, including Irish 100, 200 and 400 metres, and hurdles.

Ballymena honours Maeve for her achievements on the track, and of course the dedication she commits to developing young people's talent."

It is an appropriate place for a lasting tribute to the effervescent Kyles, but it is merely a morsel of the tale of two remarkable people, their lifestyles and backgrounds. Peeling back the layers also discloses a time-lasting love story.

Maeve was Ireland's first female athlete to compete at the Olympic Games at Melbourne, Australia, in 1956, when coached by husband Sean.

The rise to track legend though, began in Dublin for Kilkenny-born Maeve Shankey, and her natural talent was fine-tuned in Ballymena by Sean, after the pair married following a blind date in 1953.

The beginning of over half-a-century of unstinting sacrifice and devotion to athletics started with the launching of Ballymena Ladies' AC, and that early formative time included a period of training and sports days at The Showgrounds. Rapid progress resulted in a female and male club, and with that came an endless assembly line of top quality athletes, later to manifest into the all-enveloping Ballymena and Antrim AC at Antrim Forum.

The boundless enthusiasm of the livewire and optimistic Kyles helps provide a magical mirror of Irish sport, and also their experiences when daily living was less frenetic. They were born and reared 250 miles apart, and in contrasting environments during a forgiving idyllic time - a golden age of special innocence.

The storytelling of Sean and Maeve Kyles' great adventure, one that includes serene moments, sweet success, high anxiety and gripping heartbreak, is suitably sprinkled with absorbing anecdotal recollection. The lives and times of the Kyles have never been dull, with no let-up to their ceaseless strive for perfection.

2006 marked the 50th anniversary of Maeve Kyle's historic Olympic Games debut in November 1956.

Melbourne was a defining moment in a fabulous competitive career. She broke the mould as Ireland's first female athlete to compete in an Olympic Games, and drew a special line in the sand in the Antipodes. Memories of Melbourne are paramount, but there are many telling and wonderful experiences enacted before and after November 1956 to make fascinating recollection.

Sean and Maeve have chartered many great adventures to become legends of world athletics. Their insatiable appetite for all aspects of track and field coaching

18

and competition is richly illustrated through their unstinting devotion to the Ballymena Athletic Club [later to become the Ballymena and Antrim Athletic Club when it relocated to the Antrim Forum] a club they founded 50 years ago [as Ballymena Ladies AC].

The Kyle story is a unique legacy for Irish sport, and not just athletics. From the ecstasy and agony that often come in equal measure from competition to the uneasy entrance to Northern Ireland athletics and hockey after Maeve moved 'north' to become Mrs Sean Kyle.

From the recounting of the dramatic rise to top-flight hockey prowess, reaching global acclaim as one of the world's all-time great wingers of international ladies hockey, to the recollection of an extraordinary love story from the moment the Kyles met on a 'blind date' at the now defunct Hall's Hotel in Antrim.

But, let's begin the yarn by peering into the past before the Kyle-Shankey alliance.

Groundings In The Heartland

John Noel Kyle was born on December 28, 1926, in Ballymena, the heartland of County Antrim's rich farming community. The rustic background, even in such a conservative township, was to provide an enduring understanding of broad and basic living values.

He has always been known as Sean, a name given to him by his mother Dorothy.

"My father's name was John Kyle and there were a number of Johns working for the family so, because of the proliferation of Johns around the place, my mother called me Sean. She also occasionally referred to my brother James as Seamus," explains Sean.

"I was always Sean, and it never gave me any problems. Many people down South first thought Maeve Shankey married a Catholic. On the other side of the story, many people in the North thought I married a Catholic from Kilkenny. They were all wrong.

I also recall further confusion. I was attending a rugby international in Dublin and a group of fans in front of me in the stand at Lansdowne Road happened to be discussing the marriage of Sean and Maeve. They were convinced Maeve married the distantly related Jack Kyle, the rugby star. It is funny the presumptions some people have."

Sean continues an acute perception of all things earthy and balanced, and retains an abiding distaste for deceptions and charlatans. Quite often, his ethical approach in matters of athletic importance often pushed the debate to the edge of verbal confrontation down the years.

Never one to shirk from what he perceives is honesty and truth, his precise but flexible Presbyterian family background always seeks out an acceptable level of fairness.

Sean's business and sporting adventures span the pre-War times of unhurried living to the present day's more frantic lifestyles. His succinct recollections also include some

Sean Kyle, 1947

anecdotal evidence that help to illustrate many historic facts about the growth of the prosperous town of Ballymena.

During his 'short-pants' period, Sean's recollections suggest school bookwork was an understandable daily drudge as he became drawn to activities of a sporting nature. It is no surprise to find out where the seeds of interest in athletics were sown, and led to global status as a top coach.

Now retired, as a director of the 1879-founded family firm of John Kyle & Son - Insurance Brokers, Property and Rent Agents, Sean was one of three children.

Sean and his father, John Kyle

21

Born and bred in Ballymena, there was a liberal tradition in the family. His mother's family name was Skillen and her younger brother Graham played rugby for Malone.

Sean was the youngest of the family. The eldest was his sister Dorothy, who became one of the first 'GI' brides in the British Isles, and possibly the first out of Northern Ireland.

Dorothy married Wade Meintzer, a member of the American 82nd Airborne Division. He was of German extraction, and his mother was an original pioneer of the real Wild West along the Oregon Trail.

Sean's brother James became a doctor, and ended up Chairman of the British Medical Association. He lives in retirement in Scotland, overlooking the Isle of Skye.

James & Sean Kyle, 1935

Ballymena Academy 1st XV, 1943

22

As Sean recalls; "James was not into sports, as he had a problem with his chest. Parents in those days were worried about kids suffering consumption. Nonetheless, James was certainly very interested in sport, but not allowed to play rugby. My sister had the beauty, and my brother had the brains."

Rugby was Sean's first sporting priority at school. He attended Ballymena Academy from 1932 to 1944, after winning a Fullerton Scholarship. He passed Junior and Senior Certificates with a variety of distinctions. He played in the Medallion XV and was in the team that reached the semi-final of the Ulster Schools' Cup against Belfast Instonians, only to lose in the dying minutes of the game.

John Kyle & Sean, 1953

"We lost to a penalty goal by "Kipper" McKibben, kicked from the touchline in the last minutes of the game, and we went out 9-8. That was one of my first heartbreaking setbacks in sport."

From schools rugby, Sean moved to Ballymena Rugby Club, at their new post-War base at the rear of The Showgrounds.

Sean & Vanguard, 1953

"I was the original match-secretary, and played centre and wing for the club. The Club had so little money in those days that I used to have to go on my bicycle or on my feet to deliver notices. We could not afford the postage. Basically, at that time we were all things to all people, as we were during the Wartime days. We did everything. We used to go around the Young Farmers' Club sports days in the summer time, and compete in everything from the 100 yards upwards."

Sean & Mother at RDS, 1953

23

Ballymena Academy 1st XV, 1944

Sean is the last surviving of the three people who helped to reorganise the Ballymena Rugby Club after World War Two. The others were the late Tom Bloomer of the Waveney Laundry and the late Paddy Owens, who was a seed merchant in Ballymena.

The Club was placed in abeyance from 1939, and the three musketeers decided to resurrect it.

The team played at the wee Showgrounds, the lower park - and being Joint Secretary, along with his father, of the County Antrim Agricultural Association, Sean was able to secure access to the playing pitch.

Their first match was in the winter of 1944/45, a friendly against Ballymena Academy, on a Wednesday afternoon as early closing day for shops in Ballymena was then a Wednesday - and most of the people who were involved in the rugby club were free on that day. The team ended up as the premier squad of Ballymena Rugby Club.

Ballymena originally played at the Demesne, where the Seven Towers Leisure Centre is presently located, and the pitches used during the early 1940's were just behind where the Waveney Hospital once stood, on the Cushendall Road.

Sean's abiding interest in athletics had a good foundation at school, before his sporting commitment switched to rugby. Then it was back to full focus on athletics, and trying to form Ballymena Athletic Club.

Preparing for the Ballymena Agricultural Show, 1952

As a child, he was involved in the high jump, and was the school record holder in 1944 - a feat lasting until 1965. He won a bronze medal in the Northern Ireland schools' high jump event, and was also in the school's relay teams - for 110 yards and 220 yards. He also participated in school cricket, lawn tennis, and table tennis teams.

His career, as a sports person and respected businessman, is deeply embedded into the fabric of Ballymena life. After holding a fact-finding chat with the late Paddy McQuillan, a butcher and publican in Ballymena, he discovered there really wasn't an organised athletics club in the town.

McQuillan, also a noted sportsman and low handicap golfer at Ballymena's Raceview and at Cushendall, could relate strong athletics action in Ballymena around the 1912 to 1914 era.

Great runners and jumpers arrived from the South to compete in the athletics meeting. The City of the Seven Towers was but a sleeping giant as far as athletics was concerned, but Sean and Maeve Kyle were to stoke the embers.

There was always a great sporting tradition in Ballymena. Senior citizens of the Town invested a certain amount of money to set up a Recreation Company around 1885, and that is why elderly people in the Harryville area of Ballymena still talk about going to 'The Rec', rather than the Showgrounds.

The Ballymena Showgrounds facility was originally known as the Recreation Grounds. At the bottom corner of the complex was a double pond, with a diving pool and a swimming pool. There was also a boating lake in the area, where the sheep exhibits are now held.

Sean with his father John Kyle, receiving M.B.E., Mother Dorothy and brother James, Buckingham Palace, 1965

In the section where the dog sheds and dog-judging rings used to be was Ballymena's first Bowling Green.

The Rec also hosted archery, hockey for men and women, soccer, and occasional races for horses. Also, and it is not a widely known fact, but on the foundations of the Des Allen Suite, situated in the new Grandstand at The Showgrounds, was once the first prominent 500 metres cycling track in Europe.

It was called the Little Showgrounds, and bicycle manufacturers such as the famous Dunlop firm, sent over men from England to contest the races.

Sean meets Edward Heath, Edinburgh, 1970

The complete and varied sporting complex of Ballymena Showgrounds was there long years before clubs such as Racing Club of Lisbon, Real Madrid of Spain or Racing Club of Paris picked up the idea.

There was a twin problem to consider regarding this revolutionary concept, as Sean recounts; "Most of the people of Ballymena lived in Harryville, during the early days of the Recreation Club. They resided on the far side of the River, and had to come across and up the hill. It proved too far, because the Showgrounds was about a mile and a half away. Don't forget, people didn't have transport in those days, and the roads were not too good. On top of that, the thing was badly run. There were repeated financial problems.

My grandfather, James Kyle, a man of some substance at the time, was invited in to be secretary/treasurer. He was brought in to do a tidy-up operation. Everybody involved had a horse and carriage in those days, and was interested in agriculture. Out of that came the transition and development from the Ballymena Recreational Company to the Ballymena Agricultural Society, and from that situation was the founding of the Ballymena Agricultural Show. After a few years, it gained the grander title of the County Antrim Agricultural Association.

It evolved into the biggest agricultural show of its type in the entire British Isles. It was also a precursor for people to qualify for the Royal Ulster Show at Balmoral and the Royal Dublin Show.

The Ballymena Show was a massive attraction in its heyday, with well over 50,000 people going through the turnstiles to watch the one-day proceedings. Ballymena did not want to be overshadowed or overpowered by the Balmoral Show in Belfast, as Sean explains.

"Indeed, there were animals winning at Balmoral making third place at Ballymena! There was a good reason for that to happen. Local farmers could bring in their entries fresh at eight or nine o'clock on the morning of the Show, have them judged at 10am, and have the stock home by 3.30pm in the afternoon.

Whereas, if you entered for Balmoral or Dublin, the animals had to go for almost a week, and were in danger of losing weight by the time they entered the judging ring. That was also a very expensive business."

The Berlin Factor

Leni Riefenstahl, an acclaimed film producer in her native Germany during in the 1930's, was the reason why a young Sean Kyle stayed on in Belfast on four successive Wednesday evenings - after completing family insurance business in the heart of the city, in 1949.

He found it a little bit uncomfortable, and out of character, to be spending balmy summer evenings inside the long-since defunct Regal Cinema on the Lisburn Road. It was a means towards an end though, a special mission to improve Sean's education in the growing world of global athletics.

The Regal Cinema became a short-haul haven for a young and inquisitive Sean Kyle over a four-week period. It seemed incongruous this young man from the country should be rushing to the Regal to find some escapism at the 'flicks'. But, he was fascinated by four one-reelers on the controversial 1936 Olympic Games, staged in Berlin - and recorded from her own perspective by Leni Riefenstahl.

After producing the award-winning film "Triumph of the Will" in 1934, Leni took an acute interest in the Berlin Olympics - and always maintained she was just making art, and never acknowledging she was a willing participant for Adolf Hitler. The "Olympiade" went on general release, as a support to the main feature films in many cinemas throughout the UK.

29

Sean Kyle was not interested in main feature films in this instance, but logging the works of Miss Riefenstahl in his head to help set down his ground rules in relation to coaching. He was now hooked on the true essence and mechanics of athletics, and the coaching of all aspects of track and field sports.

The search for deeper knowledge led to his discovery of Riefenstahl's series of special small films depicting in detail the unique 1936 Olympic Games. This had a profound effect on him, and he remembers the significance of the film series: "It was as if I had a seat beside the track. I couldn't miss the Riefenstahl chronicles. I went to Belfast on a Wednesday afternoon to the various insurance companies, regarding claims, because my family business was as Insurance Brokers. I stayed on, went to the pictures, and took the last train home.

I was absolutely mesmerised when I saw the first of her four reels on the Olympics. I went back each week to see the remaining reels. I was gob-smacked, with stars in my eyes - coming home floating on air, after seeing the wonderful youth of the day competing in the Olympics."

Sean also wanted to know about the controversial Berlin Olympics. In those days there was little correspondence, few books, no television, and precious little news about athletics - or, indeed, about the Olympics. The trips to the cinema in Belfast were part of his early grounding.

American Olympic legend Jesse Owens held magnetic interest for the young Kyle. Blessed with astonishing ability and

JAMES CLEVELAND OWENS (b. Sept. 12, 1913, Oakville, Ala., U.S.--d. March 31, 1980, Phoenix, Ariz.), outstanding American track-and-field athlete, who set a world record in the running broad jump (also called long jump) that stood for 25 years and who won four gold medals in the 1936 Olympic Games in Berlin. His four Olympic victories were a blow to Adolf Hitler's intention to use the games to show Aryan superiority.

30

Jesse Owens' Medal ceremony for the long jump at the 1936 Olympics with Tajima, Owens and Lutz

versatility, Owens was arguably the greatest natural sprinter of all time, dominating the Games in Berlin.

"Watching Jesse Owens on the screen was a marvellous experience. It was his Olympics. I was privileged to meet the legendary Jesse at the 1960 Olympic Games in Rome. That was a fabulous experience for me. I also met the famous

31

The 1936 British team are seen here passing by a crowd giving the Nazi salute.

German ex-world heavyweight champion boxer Max Schmeling at the same Games. They were there as spectators. Schmeling was a remarkable man, a former Paratrooper who lived until 99 years of age.

The wonderment of the ability of Jesse Owens is still etched in my mind. His achievements in Berlin were phenomenal.

I also remember seeing a Pathe newsreel of Howard Whitlock winning the 50K walk for Great Britain in the 1936 Olympics. Indeed, I paid special interest when viewing the Great Britain 4x400 metres team that included Godfrey Rampling, father of film star Charlotte Rampling.

That team beat the Americans to win the gold medal, and the Reifenstahl film is probably the earliest recollection I have of seeing international athletes in action. The four films had lasting impressions on me. I was always interested in movement, and to this day I would stop when walking down a street and watch a cat about to spring. I remain fascinated how a cat actually sums up the effort first of all, and then makes the launch to attain a window ledge."

Sean's interest spread to making a study of other animals, such as leopards and horses - and then trying to apply the styles and skills to coaching athletics. Members of the Agricultural Association were, at one time, allowed to school their horses for a few days after Ballymena Show, before putting the grounds back into order again to make it ready for the football season, starting a month later.

Sean recalls: "For around four days you could bring in horses for schooling, if you were a member of the County Antrim Agriculture Association. I remember going up there to pay men's wages, and sometimes I'd hang around watching the show jumpers being schooled. The late Jack Bamber had a whole range of horses there. The Bambers were very prominent in the horse business.

Willie John McBride 1974 Lions' Tour

I recall watching when he leaned over the fence and asked: 'What do you think, young man?' I said – 'I like the grey.' 'But,' argued Jack, 'that horse is a complete novice.' He then called his brother, Dr Maurice Bamber, and said: 'Take the grey over the fences.' And the horse sailed over the jumps like a dream, onto the double bank, changed his feet as it came off the single bank correctly.

Jack said: 'Right enough you have something going there. I hadn't thought a great deal about using the grey.'"

The Bambers took the grey to Dublin, and it won the Irish Novice Championship. Masserella of Italy later bought the horse for the Italian team.

33

Sean recalls seeing the horse again; "I was at the Olympics [Mexico 1968] where I saw that very same horse, all the way from Ballymena, as part of a medal-winning Italian team! I tell the yarn to illustrate how I was so captured by the movement of the horse at the Showgrounds. It was the way he went for the fences, his general attitude."

This eye for spotting talent has been transferred successfully to athletics, with Sean admitting even when there could be one thousand youngsters participating at the Antrim Forum, going through all sorts of events, it is often prospects down the line that catch his eye; "It may not necessarily be the winner of a race, or some other discipline, that attracts my attention. Often it can be the second, third, or even fourth-placed kid who is the potential for the future I would pick out, as a coach - because I liked the movement, the attitude.

To a degree, watching horses at Ballymena Showgounds - and all the graceful powerful movement involved, helped me in a small way to coach athletes. It is all about movement co-ordination, a summation of forces. You can see a flowing movement, one that is not forced, and one that is natural, instinctive.

This applies to all sports. I had some athletes at the Club, who would have trained people like Maeve into the ground. Yet, when it came to the tensions of competition they couldn't handle it."

Sean was now totally absorbed in athletics and becoming less and less involved in rugby affairs, unlike Ireland rugby legend Willie John McBride whose first sporting competition, Sean recalls, was not in rugby.

"Willie John won the Northern Ireland schools' pole-vault championship. He was at Ballymena Academy at the time. He didn't start to play rugby until his last year at the Academy. Before that he was a pole-vaulter. I also coached Willie John as a shot putter and as a discus thrower!

He could have reached Great Britain standard in both those events, but was wooed away to rugby football."

Blind Date

Sean Kyle's concentration was wayward as he steered the sandstone-coloured Standard Vanguard family car back towards Antrim, following an Ulster rugby league game at Dungannon. He was not paying a great deal of attention to the excited post-mortem held by his passengers. It was Saturday evening, March 7, 1953, and a day of destiny. He was excited, and at the same time apprehensive - wondering what he had let himself in for.

He agreed to a blind date meeting with some international hockey player from County Kilkenny. Sean was part of Ballymena rugby team players attending a dance at Hall's Hotel, one of the great social centres of another age - an original ballroom of romance.

Here's his take on that defining day: "I was playing wing for Ballymena, and that fateful afternoon at Dungannon we were involved in a Cup match. We won. Little did I know then I was heading into another match, a very special one! On that same day, Maeve was playing for Ireland in a hockey international against Scotland, at Bladen Drive, Belfast. Our common friend, between Maeve and myself, was Pat Dinsmore, who was playing left back on the Irish women's hockey team.

One of my best pals was Frank Dinsmore, Pat's brother. Amazingly, Frank's granddaughter and our granddaughter are best friends! The Blind Date was

Early days

arranged, and agreed - and we were all to meet at Hall's Hotel in the centre of Antrim Town, at eight o'clock. The girls were late, as I recall. Maeve was in a car that had a puncture on the way down from Belfast. They arrived about five minutes to nine. There was the weekly 'Hop' at the hotel, and this sounds very corny, but true - the band was playing 'Some Enchanted Evening' as Maeve walked in the door."

The world was gradually coming to terms with the new optimistic age after World War Two, emerging from the darkness of that disaster when Sean Kyle and Maeve Shankey met for that first time. Sport was slowly but surely inching back to become a form of escapism from the ghastly happenings of 1939-1945. People were beginning to go on the move again, with petrol rationing at an end.

The meeting of Maeve and Sean happened two days after the death of dictator Joseph Stalin, ending his 29-year-rule of the Soviet Union. Perhaps the most exhilarating global achievement of 1953 was that of New Zealander Edmund Hillary and Nepalese Sherpa Tensing Norga becoming the first to reach the top of the world, the summit of Mount Everest. Also, Gordon Richards, at last, won the Derby.

In the universal sporting world, former world heavyweight champion James J Jeffries died on March 3 - a year Rocky Marciano was at the height of his punching powers. For ardent followers of athletics, March 28 marked the death of tragic native-American Olympian Jim Thorpe. 1953 also illustrated the magic of iconic American golfer Ben Hogan, who secured the Grand Slam - the US Masters, US Open and British Open.

Fittingly, there was a match made in heaven, with kindred spirits about to join forces to make a massive and lasting impact on track and field athletics. The contrived introduction of Sean and Maeve at Hall's 'hop', leading to a whirlwind romance and marriage, had an interesting setting … merely a few hundred yards from the site that would later be developed into Antrim Forum.

Maeve still marvels at the special occasion, and how she was lured from Dublin to settle in the heart of County Antrim: "There was a party arranged for the girls after the international hockey match, and, believe it or not, it was my first time to attend such a do! I selected him (Sean). John Mole was the other man, just back from serving in the Korean War. Everyone got a girl, and vice-versa. It was just a hop, yet quite formal in a way.

So, as arranged, I met Sean for the first time at Hall's. This fellow had a car, a young man with a car - wowee!

After the dance, we were sitting outside the Dinsmore house at Kells, in the middle of the night, and I said to Sean 'it has turned very cold, can you turn on the heat in the car?' only to be told, 'there is no heater'. I like to repeat that memory and the date, March 7, 1953.

Next day, we went to Bangor to see some of Sean's friends. This was suddenly turning into something very serious. Sean proposed to me. I went back to Dublin, and the next thing was - I received phone call after phone call after phone call."

According to Sean it wasn't all one-sided, and there was also something special about their romance; "Maeve also did some calling on the phone, I can tell you it wasn't all one way. It was an exciting time. We had a long-range courtship, and there was a sort of telepathy between us. I recall

One for the wallet . Photo given by Maeve to Sean

sitting in the pictures at Ballymena and saying to the boys from the rugby club I must rush home. I'd leave the cinema before the end of the film, and as I was heading towards our house the telephone would be ringing as I entered the door. It would be Maeve on the blower from Dublin - that happened several times."

"Mind you," adds Maeve, "When I was introduced to this fella' I was told he was 'the biggest rake in Northern Ireland'. Are you sure you really want anything to do with him, I asked myself? I thought at the time it could be interesting. We decided to get married, after meeting merely five times. How about that!"

Sean and Maeve were engaged in August 1953. Maeve worked her notice as a teacher at Alexandra College in Dublin, and on February 24, 1954, Sean Kyle married Maeve Shankey at Howth, Church of Ireland parish church.

St. Lawrence Parish Church, 1954

38

Birth Of A Dynasty

Curiously, Maeve's links to County Antrim began long before she fell in love with Sean Kyle and moved to Ballymena. Her connection stretches back to her grandmother Shankey, and her visits to Cushendall.

Parkmore Railway Station is no longer listed on the map, nor is the old single gauge railway track from Ballymena - although the outline of this early 20th century link to the fabled Glens of Antrim, and a line of transportation through to Belfast, and beyond, is still recognisable in parts, running alongside the main road artery.

The Parkmore halt, at the top of Glenariff, is no more, however. The end of the line was a few miles further on, and was a goods-only stop that carried the strange name of Retreat House. The crumbling edifice remains situated high up on the southern slope of Glen Ballyeamonn, with a panoramic vista across the shimmering sea of Moyle to Scotland's Mull of Kintyre. It was close to the final destination for the grandmother of Maeve Kyle.

This was a little piece of heaven for Mrs Shankey, who stepped exhausted off the train at Parkmore, heavily pregnant. Goods were taken off the single gauge railway system at Retreat - and more than likely the lot jarveyed in a jaunting car down the glen to the seaside holiday town of Cushendall by goods and people transporters of that time - Alexander and Daniel O'Hara.

Maeve's father
Carrodus Gilbert Shankey

Maeve's Uncle
Harry Thrift

Twelve times Mrs Shankey inexplicably made the marathon maternity mission from her home in Dundalk to Cushendall. All of her children were born at Cushendall, and not unlike a lot of puzzlingly unpredictable happenings attached to the fascinating antecedents of Maeve, no reason can be discovered why the journeys were made.

She lived until 92 years young, never needed to wear glasses, and said her prayers in Irish until the day she died.

"I tried to find out who the people were who helped Nanna bring her 12 children into the world, and why she went to Cushendall for all the births.

"My father lived at Dundalk in his young days, as did all members of his family - yet all born at Cushendall. The late Ballymena solicitor and Glens historian Jack McCann was able to uncover a little something of my father's origins in the Glens' of Antrim. My grandmother, on my father's side of the family, originally came from County Donegal. The surname was McCarrity, and they were Protestants living in the Glens. Jack McCann searched through Layde Graveyard, outside Cushendall, but didn't really find any substantial trace of relatives. So, things remain vague," admits Maeve.

"I know little about my father's family, because he also knew precious little himself, about his brothers and sisters. This may seem strange. He never met two of them, as they emigrated before he was born. Two more emigrated later on. There were four girls in my father's family. They were all wanderers, adventurers."

Maeve retains a special affection for her late aunt Daisy - a lady of mystery who carried an air of authority, after mingling with aristocracy during most of her much travelled life. She was a governess in the heady world of the Czar of Russia's family, before the Revolution.

Maeve Ester Enid Shankey was born on October 6, 1928, in Kilkenny, and that connection sentimentally simmers under the surface. She is sincerely proud of her background, her upbringing during a lost time when respect was a hugely important part of life. She never fails to appreciate or undervalue the time-lasting influences that shaped her outlook on life from that unique era, when the canvas of rural living was deliciously balanced, and life moved at a relaxed pace.

Lots of things have touched on Maeve Kyle's life, but one thing that has stuck to her is that she has always been a real curiosity box! She had to know things.

Maeve aged 18 months

During her childhood in Kilkenny, she was to meet many interesting people whose influences have stayed with her throughout her life.

Brought up in a very strict Catholic town, yet, as Maeve recalls, 'a very kind town', Kilkenny was, and, as far as Maeve is concerned, still is, a most peculiar place of multi-nationals, and a highly intellectual centre.

"It did me no harm to be reared in such an environment, knowing everybody was not the same. We went to the hurling matches, proud

Maeve aged 18 years

41

to be a citizen of Kilkenny. That was the natural way it was. I was given such a good grounding, and I thought that was the way everybody lived!

It had nothing to do with differing religions.

There was so much more respect given in those days. Those formative years for me in Kilkenny were to stand to me for the rest of my life. There was also the connection with my college education, and Kilkenny. Alexandra College in Dublin was named after Queen Alexandra.

She was the wife of Edward VII, who had a Kilkenny connection. Edward often came to stay at Kilkenny Castle, when the Ormondes lived there. The Duke of Ormonde would shout down to daddy, 'Shankey come on up for a game of tennis' - and a couple of times, apparently, Edward was there. Daddy never made anything of it.

It was all that sort of background, and you knew it was peripheral to your life. It was there, it happened and it was part of the family life. It was the way it was."

1927

A PRETTY WEDDING.
Mr. C. G. Shankey and his bride, Miss E. K. Thrift, leaving Holy Trinity Church after the ceremony. A description of the wedding appears on page 10.

Fashionable Dublin Wedding

On the 22nd Dec., at Holy Trinity Church, Rathmines, Mr. Carrodus Gilbert Shankey, M.A., B.E., Headmaster of Kilkenny College, youngest son of Mr. Robert Shankey, Mountain View, Dundalk, was married to Miss Enid Kathleen Thrift, M.Sc., second daughter of Professor W. E. Thrift, S.F., T.C.D., T.D.

The church had been beautifully decorated with white chrysanthemums and variegated holly. The service was conducted by the Right Rev. Lord Bishop of Ossory, assisted by the Rev. Wm. Mayne, the Rev. W. Anderson, and the Rev. E. C. Hodges.

The bride wore an ivory ring velvet gown, embroidered in silver, opening over an underdress of silver tissue, and she was given away by her father.

Her veil, which was of net, was arranged with a narrow coronet of orange blossom. She carried a bouquet of white carnations and white heather, the gift of the bridegroom.

There were two bridesmaids, Miss Vera Thrift and Miss Eileen Stone, who wore apricot frocks with tight velvet bodices and floating petals of georgette and Dutch caps in georgette and velvet. They carried bouquets of pink carnations, the bridegroom's gifts to them being a gold signet ring and a gold brooch. Mr. T. H. Blackburn acted as best man, and after the ceremony a reception was held at the Royal Hibernian Hotel by the bride's mother, who wore a gown of cyclamen georgette under a coat of broadtail velvet. The bridegroom's mother wore a gown of black velvet under a black sealskin coat.

During the afternoon Mr. and Mrs. Shankey left for Switzerland, the latter wearing a fur-trimmed coat of beige chenille cloth over a frock of electric blue chiffon velvet, with a close-fitting blue hat.
(Trousseau by Slyne & Co., Ltd.).

Brian and Dermot on the River Nore, Co. Kilkenny

Maeve's father, Carrodus Gilbert Shankey, was the Headmaster of Kilkenny College when, an always curious baby, daughter Maeve began crawling around their massive three-storey house in the college grounds.

Born in 1888, he lived in the school. Later, when numbers became too great, the College was moved to Newpark, on the Castlecomer Road.

"I was given a good grounding in education and also in sport. I met so many distinguished people when I was so young I thought that was the way everybody lived! Bishop Connor, Bishop Day or Bishop Phair played golf on a Saturday with my father. They were the best of friends, all coming from various religious persuasions. There was a special ecumenical spirit around Kilkenny in those early years, long before the word became fashionable. My father also played golf quite often with our family doctor - Dr Drennan. These were men who were held in huge respect in the town, by everybody. It had nothing to do with their religion. There was so much more respect given in those days - respect for learning, respect for kindness. Unfortunately, we cannot turn back the clock to that wonderful period.

But my parents were marvellous, yet they were totally different - opposites. Daddy was quite austere, quite autocratic - and he was also pragmatic; we lived beside the river and we had to be able to swim so that we were free to play without constant supervision. So daddy took us out on the river in the canoe, and gently dropped us in! We quickly learnt to stay afloat, but we were not scared because he was there for us.

I believe we all learnt to face challenges with the same attitude – brave, but not afraid.

Incidentally, it seems at one stage in his life my dad was mistaken for Michael Collins. He looked like him, and was close to being taken out and shot by a group of soldiers.

From the time I could stand, he took me for a walk every day. There were rules in the house, yet you had loads of free space. At breakfast, you stood behind your chair until father pointed to one of us and said, 'Say grace, please' - and it had to be said in Latin. Things like that was commonplace during my upbringing. It was just the way it was. You had to mind your manners. You were taught manners very early on in life, taught to respect others. I really didn't realise I was a girl until I went to Alexandra College in Dublin at 10 years of age, because the school was all girls.

I did not know any other girls when I was little. I was brought up in an all-male society in the school in Kilkenny , where the only other females I came across, when I was small, were my mother and the maids. The fact I lived in such a society that was so very ordered and orderly, rubbed off on all of us. Sean and I came from interesting families, but did not realise it at the time. You don't notice your family is any different from any other."

The Shankey family left Kilkenny in 1953, when Maeve's father retired, at 65. Her mother wanted to go back to Dublin, where she came from, believing she would know everybody there when she went back. She didn't. Maeve's father wanted to be able to look at the sea, because he loved sailing, after being raised at Carlingford and Blackrock, outside Dundalk.

They needed a house that was big, because the only furniture they had from Kilkenny was enormous. So, a large house at Howth was purchased for £2,000 - although it was a place that was overgrown. It had a little lodge beside the house, a bungalow type building later to be converted into a town house.

The family's general factotum, Kathy Purcell [the nursemaid] who was from a place called Stoneyford, came up from Kilkenny with the family, and stayed for around five years.

However, the running of the house became very hard work for Maeve's mother. It was simply too big. So, the Shankeys moved into a bungalow, further up the hill at Howth, in 1960. Three years later Maeve's father passed away.

44

Nanny Katty and Silver

Incidentally, Maeve places a healthy influence on her formative years with Kathy Purcell: "Katty was a very important person in our lives. She was the daughter of the head Laundress in Kilkenny College, and came to live in our family when I was about four. She was minder, extra big sister, mother and teacher. Our parents were always on duty, so Katty was in charge of the "oldest children"...all three of us, like steps of stairs. Deirdre is nine years younger than me, and John (died as a toddler) was five years younger.

Katty was a lovely country girl. We loved her and totally respected her. She took us to see the cribs at Christmas, to dance at the cross-roads platform, and was

45

with us on every summer holiday - as housekeeper, nursemaid, minder and playmate.
She went to Howth to continue looking after the family...especially the "child" (my sister Deirdre) whom she had been with since she was born. Katty went back to Kilkenny. I visited her in her lovely little home in Patrick Street. She also got to know Shauna, which was great."

Larger Than Life

While Maeve's own life has been full of adventure, her kid brother Brian was something of a foot-loose adventurer who followed the family trait. It was also typical Brian's globetrotting should find romance while well lubricated - also hopelessly and embarrassingly jammed in a trashcan on a side street in Vancouver.

Weekends off work meant flying to Vancouver, where he sometimes over-indulged. His mischievous mates stuck him in the street dustbin as a joke. He was left there, unable to extricate himself. Eventually, an English born society girl, who was walking down the street at the time, helped him out of the predicament.

With typical Shankey-Thrift bravado, he brought a new meaning to being out on the town - a night on the tiles. He was so relieved to be rescued from the red-faced situation by a passing female, he instantly made a proposal of marriage to his rescuer. Amazingly, the girl accepted. It seems total madness - and by the sound bites from Maeve it was.

Brian Shankey, 1984

46

They were married soon afterwards. The girl was very talented, who had been with Constance Spry in London, and did the flower arrangements for Queen Elizabeth's wedding. She was also a niece of Lord Chief Justice Goddard. Brian later told her he would leave, once their kids were up and reared. He divorced her at 60 years of age. He now lives in Mexico.

Brian moved on to join a multi-national firm that tested hotel lifts. He designed and patented an idea for improving the tests for the Warnock-Hersey Company, retired, and settled in San Felipe, Baja, Mexico.

A bright boy, but not a serious academic, Brian was sent to university in Dublin, to study engineering. After a year, he hightailed it to South Africa. He ended up working in a gold mine, which, by an extraordinary stroke of luck, was owned by a cousin of his father, Donal Whiteside, in the Witwatersrand near Johannesburg.

Brian also secured a scholarship in mining, to attend the Witwatersrand University. His new-found career took him to Northern Rhodesia, where he took a job at the Rom Antelope copper mines, for about three years.

He became homesick one Christmas, and out of the blue arrived in Dublin. It transpired he couldn't go back however, because he had not paid some taxes.

Brian moved on to Alaska, where he was involved in the building of the tunnel that served the smelter plant at Kitimat. He was there as an engineer - and employed about a week when he declared the tunnel wouldn't meet. The owners thought he was just a mad Irishman, but he was proved right. The tunnel didn't meet, and it had to be altered - redesigned by Brian.

Dermot, Maeve's other brother, and also known for some strange reason as Mike, preferred a swash-buckling life on the ocean waves. He was the youngest Master in the British Mercantile Navy, and later he ran a Guinness boat from Dublin to Manchester before retiring to live in Dublin.

Thrift In The City

Maeve's uncle, Harry Thrift, is famous for many things during a colourful life in Dublin at the start of the 20th century, including his short-lived notoriety as the man on the bike in James Joyce's "Ulysses". More importantly, this extrovert character fits the bill as the cornerstone to a family sporting excellence, the direct blood link to Maeve Shankey.

His contributions, in high academic and athletic achievement, provide a distinctly strong strain throughout the family tree to his older brother Willie's granddaughter. Maeve can look back with understandable pride on the exploits of the enterprising Thrift brothers.

Great uncle Harry carved his own special place in Irish and Dublin folklore. He was a quality athlete, a 440 yards Irish Champion, cricketer, and cyclist - but he was better known as an international rugby winger gaining 18 Irish rugby caps, including one in the historic first visit by the New Zealand All Blacks to Dublin in 1905. He had to give up playing his beloved rugby at the early age of 23, due to a suspected heart ailment.

Both Harry and Willie Thrift were not only prominent in Dublin's high society, but both well-known figures for cycling around the city. Harry became especially famous when used by James Joyce as the man on the bike during the opening paragraphs in the original manuscript of "Ulysses". Historian John Kidd traced the rise of the inimitable Harry Thrift

NEW PROVOST OF DUBLIN UNIVERSITY.

Dr. W. E. Thrift photographed at his first official function since appointment. —(Poole, Dublin).

on his bike in the famous book to the strange airbrushing out of the saga from second edition printings.

Kidd claims: "Until his death, in 1958, Harry Thrift was known around Dublin as the man in the bicycle race in Ulysses, where he was runner-up in the quarter-mile flat handicap in the Trinity Races of June 16, 1904. Joyce doesn't mention the young man was also placed second in the first heat of the 120-yard handicap, but out of the money in the final. Ulysses is a big book, but not big enough for all the newsworthy events of Bloomsday, 1904.

The versions with H. Thrift cycling in the last segment of the "Wandering Rocks" - the only one now in the classroom - have all been replaced with versions putting an H. Shrift near the head of the pack: "Thither of the wall the quarter mile flat handicappers, M.C. Green, H. Shrift, T.M. Patey, C. Scaife, J.B. Jeffs, G.N. Morphy, F. Stevenson, C. Adderly and W.C. Huggard, started in pursuit." [1986 Ulysses, p. 209]

48

Production of all the old Thrift versions was halted in order to replace them with the Shrift version, which is claimed to be part of "Ulysses as Joyce wrote it" (1986, p. 649 and elsewhere). Did it occur to anyone to check whether Thrift was a real person before changing him to Shrift? Apparently not."

Course Capers

Rosslare remains to this day a special holiday treat, and a golfer's paradise. The links, set up in parallel with the coastline and beach, often provide a down-wind advantage one way and a stiff test into a warm summer breeze in the other direction.

This was one of the popular and obligatory summer escapes to the seaside for the Shankey family. Maeve's father and friends were all proficient golfers. Sometimes he joined famed film actor Barry Fitzgerald during holiday retreats to Dunmore East or Rosslare.

Maeve loved those the lazy, hazy wonderful days during the break from school. She was merely following an earlier pattern, set by members of the Shankey and the Thrift families. They took off with friends on mid-summer golfing junkets to various coastal centres, including Ballybunion in County Kerry and Greencastle on the Inishowen Penninsula.

Often a party of up to 20 players included Eric Scales of Belfast, a Parliamentary ecretary who was married to Maeve's aunt. Also in the party was Maeve's grandfather Willie Thrift.

Her father went to Rosslare on a fairly regular basis, to indulge in his passion for the game of golf. "Before Daddy was married, he stayed in the famous Kelly's Hotel at Rosslare, but later couldn't afford it as a family man," said Maeve.

"So, we stayed at the Iona. It was smashing fun, and always the wonderful nursemaid who looked after us would call my mother when we were leaving – 'Mrs Shankey - a little something to bring home.'

It was a fruit cake. This may seem of no significance now, but to me a little gesture of kindness like that I never forgot. Those were experiences of a very special kind. All kids remember the happy times of summer holidays, and the relating of the great adventures sometimes leant towards exaggeration when you returned to school.

I was no different. I loved going to Rosslare. There were many breathtaking escapades. My father especially enjoyed the beautiful links there. He golfed all summer long, as did my brothers and my father's friends.

Any sporting challenge was right up Maeve's street.

"At Trinity, I also did some sailing, I was reared on boats during holidays as a kid at Dunmore East" she said.

"I would be on boats, at Curabinny, in West Cork too - opposite Crosshaven. We were light and wiry as kids, my brothers and me, and we generally sailed international 14-footers.

Dad was brought up at Dundalk, and spent a lot of his youth on boats in Carlingford Lough. While he loved his golf, he was also sailing mad and we were all boat crazy. If I had been a man I'm sure I would have picked up a blue for sailing at Trinity!

My father had an enormous respect for the sea. You had to know what you were doing.

'The water and wind are always stronger than you', he would warn us - you had to learn how to handle these things. You learn so much about clouds, conditions, shadows on the water and winds. I was very much a novice, but picked up quite a lot of tips along the way."

Maeve also dabbled in cricket and lacrosse.

"Clarissa Crawford, the Warden of my Residence Hall when I was at Trinity College, was from Ballymena," Maeve said.

"She respected sport, and its values. Clarissa invited me to try cricket. I knew a little bit about the game, because, as budding tomboy I played cricket along with my brothers at school in Kilkenny. I could hit a ball, and sort of bowl - and certainly run and catch - it was the same with lacrosse. I loved it.

Nobody drove me into sport. You did it as a pastime, an activity at college. I also fished a lot back home. Our schoolteacher, Mr Hendy, taught us how to tie flies to the rod, and we fished on the River Nore for trout.

We took the fish we caught home, cooked it, put it on your plate and ate it."

The Butler

The admirable Smyton was perhaps Maeve's first inkling she was entering a whole new special level of upper class living in Dublin. In 1938, at nine years of age, she travelled from Kilkenny to Dublin to begin her advanced education, but did not join Alexandra College as a boarder until 1942. She resided with her grandparents, and, stepping off the train, was met by their butler named Smyton.

Maeve takes up the story; "He took me to my grandparents, and I lived in a big house at the bottom of Grafton Street. I never knew Smyton's first name. He was so good to me. Dressed in full regalia, he took me to school every day, through the Green - and came back for me in the afternoon. My grandfather, Willie Edward Thrift was Provost of Trinity College at the time. A well-known familiar figure in Dublin for riding a bicycle, he was a small man, and was part of the Dublin scenery, cycling down from Grosvenor Square.

Once a month, there was a special occasion - a musical afternoon at the house. It was a big social gathering, but I was not allowed in, at the start. After a year, they probably thought I had learned enough manners, so I was allowed in to sit in a corner with Patsy - my maid. There was an orchestra in the Grand drawing room. All the top social people of Dublin were there - including wives of ambassadors. It was a wonderful occasion, but I wasn't old enough to appreciate the quality of some of the minds of the people who attended this very popular function.

Some of the most unbelievable people were there, including artists - a mixture of society including politicians. I especially recall Sir Thomas Moloney, from England and a vice-Chancellor of Trinity College University. The first time I met him was after sliding down the big curved banisters, and crashing onto my bottom. It was a bit embarrassing. Sir Thomas picked me up, and asked me if I was all right. Later on, I received a card from him that included the following verses;

'Whate'er in life you undertake, and wish that you may never break

Whatever else you hope to win, pray you are not the last man in

If it is sport you care to do, steer a course that is true

Whatever game in life you play good luck be with you all the way.'

I still have that card, dated December 22, 1941. I was 13 then. To Sir Thomas I was his 'Miss Hurricane'.

We were reared to respect people, no matter who or what they were. Some meetings during that unique time in my upbringing would come back in later years.

I remember taking down a team of girls to run in the College Sports Day at College Park. The late Colin Shillington was Captain of Trinity, and invited me to send down a team - Lorna McGarvey, Irene Larkin, Susan Slinger and me.

When we were there, Eamon De Valera asked for the other girls and myself to come into the Pavilion area. Dev remembered the early days of the chess matches he used to have with my grandfather. Willie Thrift, a lovely man who died in April 1942, was also a member of the first Dail Eireann. He was a close friend of De Valera, and fought a very hard battle for secondary education in Ireland, and particularly for Protestant schools."

Maeve's first memories of her Dublin adventure include performing a delightful chore every Saturday morning, when she was sent to Fox's on the corner - near where the Molly Malone statue now stands, to get her grandfather his Fox's glacier mints.

Alexandra College, in those days, was at Earlsfort Terrace before it moved out to Milltown, where the hockey pitches were situated, during the 1980's.

Maeve's family was long connected with 'Alex'. Her grandfather was a Governor - and the whole family was educated there, all the girls.

"I was a harum-scarum "divil" when I was sent to school," admits Maeve.

52

Maeve going to school, 1940

"The opportunity arose for me to leave home, and leave my brothers - when my grandparents said I could live with them in Dublin. I didn't have to board for two years, and it also saved my parents a lot of money. It gave me the opportunity of an absolutely outstanding education.

"Having said that, I had been very well educated by my father and mother, within the school environment at Kilkenny.

It was a little bit of a wrench, nonetheless, when leaving home so young - and for a first time. There were the four of us in my family, like steps of stairs. Sadly, my youngest brother died as a toddler. I was the eldest. There was just over a year between my next brother and me, and just over a year between him and the next one of the three of us.

My father's influence was quite different on all three of us. I reacted well to what I suppose was really quite an old-fashioned autocratic type of upbringing - quite Victorian. Going to Dublin was a whole new experience altogether."

Double-up

As a pupil and teacher, Maeve's formative years were inextricably linked to Alexandra College. She looks back with warm affection; "The whole time I was at Boarding school, at Alex - my personality, my whole being as a human being, was developed through a very good system of education. There was no entrance examination at Alexandra College. I went in on scholarships. It was a fantastic school for me.

When I was there, Alexandra College also had some refugee children, and one of my friends was a Latvian girl who crossed the Baltic in a boat. I thought it was very daring to escape from Russia. There was also a big Jewish community in Dublin. The school was very cosmopolitan. I attended classes in current affairs, classes in physics, and also studied Latin, Greek and Irish for a couple of years. All this helped to shape my outlook on life.

The good Lord was also kind enough to give me a few bits of grey matter to get through college and university, and become a teacher. For my second year as a teacher at Alex I had my own Form. I was salaried. I loved teaching, and still do - nowadays transferred to my love for coaching athletics. I try to be out there helping the kids whenever I can. Perhaps my abiding interest in athletics and sport originated from my grounding in education while in Dublin. I feel I have been blessed in many ways.

Maeve teaching at Cambridge House School, Ballymena

Sport was not compulsory at Alexandra, but if you signed up you had to do it. I was right at the head of the queue to be involved in any sporting activity. I was in the hockey team that won the School's Cup . . . but the first year, when Alexandra College reached the final I wakened up on the day of the final, I couldn't turn my head, and was ruled out of the game, I had mumps. A year later, in 1946, we were in the final again, and we won the match, taking the Schools' Cup against Muckross.

That was one of many magic moments in my life, and that same year I moved on to Trinity, in October 1946.

One of my best friends from the Alex hockey team was Marion Wilson - who became Marion Crampton. She played in goal. Marion was from Cork, and had brothers who attended my dad's school. The link with Marion remained, as so often happens when you attend boarding schools.

Our daughter, Shauna went to school in Ballymena, and her best friends are from those school days. I think boarding school education is a very important moulder of character, of how you approach everything in life.

I certainly look back with great affection at my student days. It is the same ethos there now as it was when I was attending the College.

I was six years there as a student, and four as a teacher. I loved it. After that, I decided to study Science at Trinity, yet swore before that I would never teach - because both my parents taught. Both were hugely academic, both gold medallists. I had to work very hard at Trinity, and had hardly any time to indulge in sporting activities - but I had the good fortune to secure a couple of scholarships.

I managed to get an Honours Degree in Science. I finished my exams at Trinity on a Friday, started teaching on the Monday, and celebrated my 21st birthday on the following Saturday.

Also, I did not receive payment for six months. My father had no money to send me, so I found out how to make a tin of beans last a long time. I was paid after my first six months, a cheque for the sum of £60, which was a huge amount of money at that time - £10 per month.

I was also doing an Honours Diploma in Education. Those were the days, in 1950, when I was teaching until 4.30pm at Alex, and then had to shoot down to Trinity College on my bike to go in for my lectures in Education."

Coaching attentive pupils at Cambridge House

The Hockey Years

Kilkenny postman J J Gilmartin, a legendary Irish handball champion, was one of many influences on the versatile sporting skills of a young Miss Shankey. It seems an unlikely source of inspiration for the primary school pupil, who was born to carefully study all aspects of sporting excellence. Maeve was an avid learner, and involved in every sporting outlet she could find. Handball was a part of the moulding exercise that would also contribute to inner strength, self-belief and always a will to win. It was a measure of her zest for life, and her natural ability.

The quiet, good-natured Gilmartin, one of the greatest players of his generation who won the first of 10 Hardball Irish singles titles in 1936, was totally dedicated to his sport.

Maeve quickly picked up the message, and was fascinated by the strict training regime - and also the balance, power, agility and skill required for such a demanding game. Those early experiences, watching Gilmartin patiently take in endless hours of practice in the Kilkenny handball alley, lived with the wide-eyed youngster. He passed on tips on how to play handball. It was a Dawn Patrol experience.

Maeve remembers: "He was fantastic, one of the most famous of All-Ireland handball champions. As kids, we used to go down to the alley at seven o'clock

57

Alexandra College 1st XI, 1946

in the morning, hoping we'd get in some handball, and some coaching.

Mr Gilmartin would be training there, and would kindly show us how to play the game with the old hard handball. I can still feel the sting in my hands. The ball was so very sore on my young soft hands, but, I was keen to learn. The game of handball is special, I feel. It is great, because it brings in so much movement, it develops hand and eye co-ordination better than any other sport I know, and probably helped me later on in my sporting life when I concentrated on playing hockey.

I believe if you can play handball to a reasonable level, I guarantee you will be able to play any other game involving a small ball, including golf. We just played it as kids for fun, not at a competitive level. It was another game to play, and did me no harm whatsoever.

We also played tag football, the forerunner of the modern tag-rugby. I used to be sent down to the butchers to ask for a pig's bladder, to use it as a ball." Such meandering memories of early idyllic adventures in Kilkenny give an indication of how great her determination to succeed.

1st Irish Hockey Cap, 1947

The lessons learnt under Gilmartin's tutelage, proved their worth in later life as Maeve was capped 58 times for the Ireland Ladies hockey team over a 20-year period. More intriguing is the fact that this marvellously skilled and speedy player may well hold a unique record in the history of Irish women's hockey.

During a dim and distant past of a wonderful pre-television era, a 14-year-old Maeve Shankey played in the Inter-Provincial series alongside her mother Enid. Maeve retains her disarming manner of trying to make light of a seriously impressive achievement, the rarity of a mother and daughter playing representative hockey in the same team.

"I had the distinction of playing in the same side as my mother. I was in a South East team for the Inter Pro competition when I was 14, a time when I suppose there were a small number of players available - and it was not that hard to attract the attention of the selectors. My mother and I played on opposite wings in the series. The Inter Pro tournament was at low level then. It was very casual in those days. The South East team was based around the Kilkenny-Waterford area. I was roped into it, probably during the holiday times.

Mum was a very good hockey player, but did not participate at international level. She captained Trinity College when winning the Chilean Cup, and years

59

later so did I. Mum played for the "Maid of the Mountains" team in Dublin, when she resided there. Of course, she also played for Trinity College - before she went to live in Kilkenny. Mum could have been a very good player, but didn't have the opportunity, because she married, and was tied down having children."

Maeve's exploits are legend as a queen of the track, but the vibrant hockey career ranks in tandem with the high achievement in athletics. Hockey affairs take a special life in splendid isolation. It is as if there are two different people

Cardiff 1958 with Silver - Commonwealth Games

creating separate headlines.

What should not be lost sight of, is the stark fact her hockey prowess took her to Belfast, which led to the happy and everlasting love triangle between Maeve and Sean, first of all, and the full conversion to starting blocks - a devotion to athletics, and one that became index-linked with Ballymena and Antrim AC.

No matter how much she enthuses about her life, and often privileged times as a track ace, the hockey years still hold a special place in her heart.

61

England v Ireland, Wembley, 1955

"I made many friends through playing hockey. For example, I maintained a link with Betty Henderson, then Betty Kyle. She was at the Swedish Ling Institute in Dublin, doing Physical Education. We played in the same Irish hockey teams. When I came to Belfast I used to stay with Betty and her family on the Cavehill Road. Such friendships last forever. I try to carry that attitude through to Ballymena and Antrim AC," Maeve says.

She gushes when remembering many eye-catching and rewarding performances during what was really her first love in sport. Here was a period of her endlessly exciting and ever-varied sporting career when she made many lasting friendships.

"When I was 17, before I went back to Alexandra College, I was in a representative hockey team - an Irish selection against Leinster. I was selected in the Ireland team that June, just before I left school and couldn't believe it. Irish sport was seriously affected by the emergence of World War II. There was no international scene, nothing."

Blessed with natural hand and eye co-ordination, and that instinctive and exhilarating burst of speed, Maeve had the advantage over most primary school youngsters of her day in that she enjoyed a hand-me-down interest in hockey from her mother, and was taught by Mr Hendry in Kilkenny.

Ireland V England, Londonbridge Road, Dublin

The hockey stick became an instinctively strong part of Maeve's early sporting interests.

"The first bit of sports gear I ever had was when I was presented a cut-down version of a hockey stick. There was the old sticky tape you used to bind electric wires with, and this was wound around the handle of what had once been a full-sized adult hockey stick.

I was very attached to that stick, so much so I used to take it to bed with me! I worried someone might steal it. I had that stick with me when I went to Alexandra College.

There was no hockey competition at Kilkenny. Still, Mr Richard Hendy, the Art Master at Kilkenny School, taught us how to play hockey. He was a wonderful hockey tutor.

The one thing he insisted when coaching us, was that you could play nothing until you learned the skills of whatever game you were playing. That basic advice stayed with me. I learned every skill. By the time I went to Alexandra College I felt I was pretty good at hockey. You might say the stick was virtually an extension of my arm. The game came naturally to me by then. It was almost a way of life.

I absolutely loved playing hockey, yet it could lead to some frustration at times - especially when playing out on the left wing. You were terribly dependent upon other people. I was once dropped from the Irish hockey team, after playing in a game when I was not given one single pass! I felt it was so grossly unfair. After all the years, I still haven't forgotten the shock to the system."

Flying Winger

With over half-a-century of appearances for Ireland, Maeve is one of the longest serving of international hockey players. She did not train for hockey to the same degree players dedicate themselves in the present-day teams, but she practised her skills every day in Dublin - and riding a bike every day from Trinity Hall into the city centre helped to maintain a high level of fitness.

She recalls: "That was no bother, because it was downhill all the way, yet I had to ride uphill all the way back. You did that four times a day, and I tell you it certainly helped to keep me fit! We did not have a club hockey coach, as is the norm nowadays, but at international level we had Kate Russell. She wasn't a coach, but was the manager of the team. She was just Kate, and I loved Kate to bits. She was from Cork, and was a bit like my father - as I was half scared of her, but held her in total respect. She organised us in every respect."

Maeve was at Alexandra College when invited onto a Leinster team to play in an early-season unofficial game. That was during September of 1946; four months later, in January 1947, Maeve was called up to play for Ireland.

In 1950, with Maeve in the side, Ireland won the inaugural Triple Crown title. She was also in the first women's team to play at Wembley Stadium, in 1951 and in front of 40,000, in an international against England.

Maeve also had a couple of international trips overseas including visits to Holland and Belgium, and she played in the World Cup [or World Conference as it was called] at Folkestone, in 1953.

Not long after the World Conference, Sean began to coach Maeve in the finer points of athletics.

Much later down the line, in 1976, Maeve coached field hockey in Canada.

Based in Montreal, she coached the province of Quebec. At that stage Quebec had been for years the ninth and last of the provinces. Maeve took them over, and the juniors went to the top of the list the following season while the seniors moved off the bottom and into the top three.

The Canadian hockey authorities also invited Maeve to be their National team coach. However, while tempted to take up the offer, Maeve did not wish to be away from her family in Ballymena. Also a consideration was Canada is such a vast land mass, such a huge country, she could not face all the travel involved.

Rocky Road To Melbourne

Preparations to meet the demands of Olympic track tests had an unwittingly imperfect launching for Maeve. Unaware the invitation to break the mould for female Irish athletes was just around the corner; she was off on a lazy autumn break around Europe. In September of 1956, she went on holiday in Austria, and had not the slightest notion a surprise trip to Melbourne in November was in the pipeline.

She concedes: "I found myself in a bit of a bind, fitness-wise, because of the holiday. I first heard the selection news on a crackling radio bulletin! That was on the way back from Europe, after a wonderful holiday. On the way out, and it could only happen in Ballymena, I was with my husband and ten other males heading to Austria! It was kind of strange. This gang, including Sean, had very little money, mind you - yet decided on this great adventure, to go to Europe on vacation.

Nobody had really travelled much in those days. People in Northern Ireland and in Britain, generally, were getting over the War years. This was a first opportunity to go on a special break. I made all the travel arrangements. We used to get together at the Clarence Hotel in Ballymena, mainly on a Saturday evening, to have a few beers - and then back to our house for chinwags.

During one of those gatherings, the gang decided to go on a holiday, and I was asked to do the organising. I went to Greer's Travel in the town. I wanted to go as

66

Irish Team, opening ceremony, Melbourne Olympics 1956

close to an eastern Europe country as possible. I was keen to go to General Tito's Yugoslavia, but we finished up travelling to Austria. We went to Karinthia, right on the south east of Austria - a special place, nestling beside a lake.

And how did we go there? We went by the Orient Express!

It was a fabulous experience, but to get there we had to make our way to Hull, first of all, cross over the channel to Zeebrugge, and then hop on a train down to Paris. The twelve of us had dinner on the Express train. Fortunately, the boys brought jackets and ties, and we had this dinner party on the Express, as the famous train hurtled through Europe. I thought that was magic carpet stuff!

I remember swimming in this amazing lake, where the Germans once used to send their injured pilots to recover after being badly burned.

There were sulphur or skin-healing mineral salts in the water. The peculiar thing was that you would go in for a swim sporting a good suntan and came out without one!"

The holiday lasted a fortnight during which time Maeve freely admits on a diet of coffee, beer and wild strawberry torte she was fast becoming "as fat as a fool!"

67

Melbourne hosts the Olympic Games, 1956

Maeve came home totally out of condition, to find she was selected for the Olympic Games in Melbourne. The shock of it all!

The Ballymena athlete had around two months to get herself into shape.

There was no proper athletic track in the Ballymena area then, and Maeve used to do most of her training on an old cinder circuit at Ballymena Showgrounds where she'd do her fitness and speed training.

Lunchtime training involved warm ups, and a lot of laps. She also ran up and down the old disused dump at the back of her first home, in Leighinmohr Avenue.

"There were little dry cinder tracks through the dump, and it was a great place to train," explains Maeve.

"Colin Shillington, a top 800 metres runner at the time, and I trained there for ages. I was wildly excited about the great adventure of going to my first Olympics. I had Sean backing me, and Shauna, our daughter, about to have her second birthday."

Maeve taking photos, Melbourne 1956

Maeve's odyssey in Oz began with many fascinating and sometimes frustrating adventures long before achieving a special place in the history of the Games.

Her emergance from hockey to concentrate on track affairs had its roots in Dublin, but more fully fostered and patiently nurtured in Northern Ireland.

69

She was playing for Pembroke Wanderers at top-level hockey when she first tested the waters in athletics. Before joining Crusaders AC, who used the same ground at Serpentine Avenue in Dublin, there was a sports tournament in 1948 at Lansdowne Road where hockey girls were persuaded to compete.

This was where athletics really began for Maeve, if unwittingly at that time. She ran in the 110 yards, and won the high jump. Joan O'Reilly who played on the other wing in the Irish hockey team won the 110.

Maeve had no specialised training at that time, and was not programmed in any way then for track running. That was to come later, through Sean's influence. She trained all through the summer of 1948 under the guidance of Crusaders' coach Joe O'Keefe before going to Belfast to run in the RUC Coronation Sports at Ravenhill where she won the 80 yards sprint, and also the 220 yards.

That was Maeve's first attempt at serious sprinting. In those days women did not compete in distance events, just 100 and 200 metres, as they are now. The 400 metres did not surface in the Olympics for women until 1964, and the 800 metres arrived as an experiment in 1960, but just trials.

Initially, there was much opposition to Maeve's selection for the 1956 Irish Olympic team. Fairly blunt offerings of discontent came from Dublin, and mainly in the media.

Sean takes up the story: "The Ireland team never had a woman representative competing in the Olympics before then. The audacious idea of Maeve going to Melbourne created a mental hurdle for some folk. People were not used to the idea of women becoming involved, given any recognition.

She was sort of a suffragette for Irish athletics! It was considered by her critics there were several male athletes who were possibly more likely to be included in the team, more worthy than Maeve for the 1956 Games. Brendan O'Reilly, a high jumper, was mentioned."

However, the grey area surrounding O'Reilly's non-appearance in Melbourne was later clarified. The point was, Maeve came up with the necessary funding, and £200 was needed at that particular time. It was a fortune in those days.

"Maeve was well known in hockey then, and we managed to get some good times on the track for her. Once she was in the team that was it. Still, there was that uneasy period before then, I have to admit. I felt the thinking then was that any man - despite what his calibre was, would be a better and more acceptable choice than that of a woman."

70

It required exceptional performances by Mrs Kyle to convince the selectors, and secure the invitation to compete in the 1956 Olympic Games. It was a momentous milestone for female progress in Irish athletics.

The four gold medal haul at the 1948 Olympics in London by Dutch ace Fanny Blankers-Koen provided the cornerstone inspiration for women's athletics worldwide, but sadly not in Eire where it was hard to shed the shackles of conservative thinking.

The then Catholic Archbishop of Dublin, Dr John Charles McQuaid expressed his view in 1950 he felt it was unbecoming of young women to "display themselves before the public gaze" - and disapproved of the practice of allowing "young women to compete in cycling and athletics in mixed public sports".

Ironically, that same year, female athletes in Northern Ireland formed the NI Women's Athletic Association - but south of the Border ladies' athletics was taboo for a further decade.

In 1960, Trinity graduate Maeve accepted an invitation from Trinity College's captain and top Northern Ireland 880 yards runner - and also Trinity record holder, Colin Shillington to bring a team of women from Ballymena Athletic Club to compete in Dublin.

This was a groundbreaking move against the dreaded prohibition, with Ballymena members competing against members of the Irish Ladies Hockey and Tennis Clubs in College Races.

The Ballymena ladies contested the 100 yards, and also the 4 x 100 yards relay - but Maeve smashed the barrier long before that.

She was the first women's athletics champion at university and national level, Melbourne was to prove another special rung up the ladder of recognition for women's athletics.

"I remember receiving a letter from Crusaders AC Secretary Tony Caldwell, congratulating me on being selected for the Olympic Games. I was one of two athletes named for Melbourne who had a connection with the Dublin club. The other was Ronnie Delany. I don't really know exactly how it came about, my selection for Melbourne," acknowledges Maeve.

"I was running that summer in London, and alongside some breathtaking sprinting by Jean Paul (Foulds). I ran quite well in the Women's Three A's at White City in 1956, but did not win a medal or anything. I ran against Jean, who was timed at 10.6 for 100 yards.

I clocked 11.3, which wasn't really very good, but Norris McWhirter maintained at that time I was much better than that. He was doing the BBC commentary. That was in August of 1956. I won in other events before that. In 1955, I was successful in all sorts of things, improving all the time, and in really very good nick during the summer of '56. I was unbeaten locally, in all competition in Northern Ireland. This obviously was noted. I also competed in what was probably a highly significant meeting, the Edinburgh Highland Games at Murrayfield, in August 18, 1956.

Ann Pashley won the 100 yards. I was second during appallingly heavy rain - and on a grass track. She ran 11.4, and I was timed at 11.5. Ann was still the British champion - she was later to become an opera singer.

I believe that probably was the race that influenced the Irish Olympic team selectors. That counted hugely, I feel, and was the key to it all. It was, however, a strange progress for me. I had this reputation of being very fast on a hockey field, and somebody picked it up. As a result, members of the Olympic Council decided to send me. Sean coached me in all the techniques of sprinting."

Still, the rise to that first adventure as a late developing track star required that special brand of crusty Kyle tenacity. Maeve could just as easily have settled for the life of a housewife and young mother in Ballymena, but that wasn't Maeve. It wasn't her way. Six weeks after she had given birth to her daughter Shauna,

With Shauna, aged 2   *Training with Paddy Toner*

Maeve was back playing international hockey. Shauna was born in the month of November, Maeve returned to hard training in December.

"In 1956" explained Sean, "races in Ireland and Great Britain were measured in yards. Races at the Olympics, as well as the European Championship were measured in metres. Races in Ireland and Great Britain were first measured in metres during the mid 1960's"

Shadow Boxing

Ireland's Chef de Mission Christy Murphy suddenly took ill in San Francisco at the Irish boxers' training camp, ahead of the Games. He was also manager of arguably the most formidable boxing team ever to represent Ireland at the Olympics.

While Ronnie Delany led the honours list, Dublin welterweight Freddie Teidt, from the South City club, was robbed of gold against Romania's Nicolae Linca.

Bantamweight Freddie Gilroy, born in Belfast's Ardoyne district in March 1936, was a bronze medallist in that magnificent seven-man side. It fell to 'big sister' Maeve to look after the Irish team, as Belfast boxing legend Freddie Gilroy explained;

"When we arrived in Australia we had no manager. However there was an Irish fellow who lived in Melbourne, Snowy Sullivan - and he joined to help us in the corners during the contests. It was Maeve Kyle who looked after our interests in most instances. She always kept an encouraging eye out for the boxing team members. Maeve was marvellous. She maintained a special watch over us - in what we ate, to make sure our diet was right, and in how we trained - even though she was in a different department.

The 1956 national champion recalls the many incidents: "It was some adventure, I tell you - the whole trip, right from the moment we started out from Shannon Airport, and headed to New York. We stopped off in San Francisco for training, while the athletes went to LA," he said.

"We worked out really hard in a gym in San Francisco, and stayed there for a week. On a day off, away from the gym, we were taken on a trip outside the City by the Bay - to visit a cowboy ranch. Tony Byrne jumped on a horse. 'Socks,' an amazing character - always buzzing, was a baker down in Drogheda, and claimed he was used to working with a horse and cart. This was different, however.

The horse was hard to control, reared up in the air, and Tony was thrown from it. That was the moment when Christy Murphy, who was with us, took suddenly ill, and was rushed into hospital! We continued to train in a pro gym, and sparred with

73

Maeve and the Irish Boxing Team, Melbourne 1956

professionals, mostly from Mexico. We worked out with five top professional fighters. An American trainer in the gym remarked - "After such good performances in sparring, when you gave my boys a right going over, if you Irish don't win medals there will be something wrong at the Olympics.

I must say we all looked sharp, and from those training sessions in San Francisco we were well tuned in. There was certainly a belief in the boxing squad, that we could take home medals - and that is the way things worked out. But it was awkward at times, with Christy Murphy unwell"

The boxers made a huge contribution to the whole Irish enterprise, and Maeve holds a special fondness for them as she recalled her unexpected role of 1956; "They were all younger than me, so I was the older sister in our little family...helping out where I could making sure they maintained a healthy diet...ironing the odd shirt, or just chatting to make them feel not so far away from home.

They were a fabulous group of young men, who took the chance of recognition through their ability and commitment to a tough sport. They hadn't had the same opportunities in life that I had, and I admired them greatly."

Tony Byrne, the 1956 Irish amateur lightweight champion, boxing out of the Tredagh Club, went on to win bronze from the Games. His recurring ring adversary, southpaw Scot Dick McTaggart, took gold. Belfast Immaculata club's Johnny Caldwell, who retained his 1956 Irish flyweight title before turning professional and later won a version of the world bantamweight championship, also bagged bronze. Completing the fighting Irish were national featherweight Martin Smith, a 1955 bantamweight champion from the Belfast Star club. The fabulous Harry Perry, a nine-times Irish champion from the Dublin British Railways club at light-welterweight, and heavyweight Pat "Pa" Sharkey at light-heavyweight. Sharkey lived in Australia at that time. He was from Donegal, and was a former Ulster and Scottish champion.

Track Trauma

If looking after the boxing team's needs as well as her own preparations weren't enough for Maeve, a moment of madness, when an overzealous Olympic trackside official questioned Maeve's sex, almost ruined the dreamtime Down Under. Competing at the Games was perhaps the pinnacle of her career, a momentous groundbreaking appearance - yet it might never have happened. Before being wrong-footed, literally, she tried to overcome a bout of nerves, appearing to be calm and composed during the warm-up to her historic debut.

The memorable moment for Ireland's first female Olympian almost turned to disaster when she was curtly instructed to prove her female gender. She was in the process of completing her warm-up on the track, the great occasion just around the corner - and almost ready to make the starting line for 100 metres qualifying.

Maeve takes up the story: "Before the starter's pistol was fired, I was naturally nervous, but this was too much on my Olympic debut. I became very angry! It was a shattering setback, awful - and certainly no way to help me make my first appearance in an Olympic Games."

Maeve was hopping mad when told she would not be allowed to run - and that shocker was merely moments before the first heat was about to start on November 24, 1956.

Maeve and Ronnie Delany in San Francisco, 1956

She was told she had to undergo a sex test. "I felt everyone in the Stadium was looking at me. It was so confusing, so embarrassing. I was out on the track when an official barked out instructions to me - Kyle out. I asked what the problem was. I was told I had not passed the sex test. I confirmed to the official I did not have and had not been previously asked to undergo a sex test. I was informed there was no certificate to prove I was a female. My manager did not leave in the certificate. I told them we had no manager, because he took ill on the way out to Australia.

Fortunately, we sorted out the thorny and aggravating issue. I was allowed to run - just in time, but I came up against too much class. I failed to qualify. World record holder Betty Cuthbert was in our heat, and with one athlete to qualify and a couple of fastest losers. I had a poor start to the 100 metres, in every possible way. On top of the sex-test drama, I must confess I had a bad attack of nerves. Two days later I ran in the 200 metres. I just wasn't fast enough.

I have to confess I did not do anything worthwhile at the Olympics." [Maeve clocked 12.48secs for sixth place in the first round of the 100 metres, and 26.57secs for fifth place in the first round of the 200 metres].

1956 Irish Team in Dublin

"I was unlucky to draw the world record-holder in my heat. I wasn't in that league of Margery Jackson and Betty Cuthbert. Still, I am proud I was a bit of a pioneer, as the first woman to compete for Ireland on the Olympic track. I drew Betty Cuthbert in one of the heats, and Heather Armitage in the other - and also crack Australian Shirley Strickland de la Hunty, a nuclear physicist, who won seven gold medals from three Games. Still, I was there, and did my level best. Maeve Kyle was the most astonished and delighted person in the world to be sent to Melbourne."

The 1956 Olympics will always be warmly remembered in Ireland as the Ronnie Delany experience of a special kind, a majestic milestone in the history of Irish athletics.

Many regard Delany as the best track talent ever produced on this island. He became the second Irish track ace to win Olympic gold, following Bob Tisdall's historic 400 metres hurdles victory of 1932 at Los Angeles. In the Melbourne 1500 metres final, the ten runners included six who previously smashed the four-minute mile barrier. Delany left it tantalisingly late, coming from 10th with 300 metres remaining.

78

He sensationally covered the last 100 metres in 12.5 seconds, to finish well ahead of Germany's Klaus Richtzenhain and the host nation's favourite John Landy.

Delany is forever remembered at the Melbourne Cricket Ground, where his spikes remain on show in the club's museum. The former Irish schools' 880 yards champion, a record holder from the Irish 880 yards senior title in 1954 at College Park, made his first major move when competing in the European championships at Berne, Switzerland. He reached the 800 metres final, and also broke the Irish record in the process.

Ronnie received a scholarship offer to join Villanova under their coach Jumbo Elliott. A year later, he ran his first mile for the legendary Billy Morton, and clocked 4:5.8 at College Park. He continued to run at 880 yards, and also 440 yards in the States, but began to concentrate more and more on running the mile distance. He eventually broke the barrier in California on June 1, 1956, and became Ireland's first sub-four minute miler in a time of 3 minutes 59 seconds. Once selected for Melbourne, Ronnie had his final workouts in California.

Maeve was amazed how much improvement Ronnie achieved since switching to a college grooming in the United States.

"I remember writing a letter to Sean from Los Angeles, after the track meeting at Berkeley University on our way out to Australia. I stated then - whoever beats Ronnie will win the 1,500 metres gold at the Games. He didn't run much in Ireland, and did most of his races in the States," she said.

"He is a great friend of mine. When I toppled over with a heart problem, in the summer of 2004, one of the first telephone calls to wish me well was from Ronnie Delany, all the way from Spain, where he was on holiday. When told I had taken ill, Ronnie immediately took the trouble to ring me, again proving to be such a very close personal friend.

I worked with him when he was Chairman of the Irish Sports Council. He was excellent. All those years ago he set a lofty standard for Irish running. But, for some strange reason he didn't seem to be given the proper credit or respect back home. A bit of the old prophet not listened to and accepted in his own land, perhaps."

Sean's view confirms the contradictions in the sporting life of his good friend, the legendary Delany: "Ten years after Melbourne, we asked him to give a motivational talk for our kids at the Bearís Club in Gormanstown, on a Saturday night - and 300 youngsters were left in awe of this great athlete. The Bear's Club was an unofficial thing, yet about the first coaching organisation in Ireland. Ronnie was a huge success.

I recall him saying, at that time, how delighted he was to make a speech - because it was the first time he had ever been asked in Ireland to say anything as an Olympic Games gold medallist. I found that amazing, incredible, that the great Ronnie Delany was never asked to do anything during the ten years after his historic record-breaking run in the Melbourne!"

Maeve pondered on the anomaly: "We used to be a very insecure people, no sense of self-esteem. If somebody broke through, was good, was a winner, they almost pulled you down! It still baffles me. Ronnie is a very personable man, with huge experience of all sports.

One of his biggest contributions, quite apart from the 1500 metres breakthrough in Melbourne, was he made absolutely certain a lot of our young people realised that going to an American university was a way to the top.

He was a trail blazer in that regard, one of a kind on the track in America, and at the same time showed you could secure a good education while you were doing athletics. He was one of the early ones to go to the States.

After the London Olympics of 1948, the American University experience began to open up. Jimmy Riordan, a 400 metres finalist in 1948, and another Donore Harrier's athlete Cummin Clancy - who was the British AAA discus champion in 1948, were offered scholarships to Villanova University, near Philadelphia.

A year after that, the great middle-distance runner John Joe Barry went there. They opened up the strong Irish connection at Villanova. Ronnie followed. He also gave people a belief, and proved we could take on the world, and win. His was a massive victory in Australia, and it shot Irish sport to the top of the world, from parochial to international.

Bob Tisdall and Pat O'Callaghan also won Olympic gold before that, yet I felt Ronnie was different. The history of sport often reflects the times in respective countries. Every sport produces a winner here and there, and always will, but there was no consistency here. In recent years we had a better level of consistency than then, one that ran almost parallel to the rise of the Celtic Tiger - rugby, and other sports, producing winners like never before."

Flight Of Her Life

1956 was a leap year, and a very eventful one at that. The Hungarian Revolution started in October, and on November 4 Soviet troops invaded Hungary. The other global concern was the Suez Canal crisis that led to the Egyptian government's blocking of the canal on November 16. Gamal Abdel Nasser of Egypt (1918-1970), a pivotal figure in the modern history of the Middle East, played a highly prominent role in the 1956 Suez crisis when he challenged what was perceived as the western dominance of the Arab world. Nasser nationalised the canal - provoking an attack on Egypt by the French and British. This attack was condemned at an international level, and the British and French had to withdraw their forces, when it became clear America did not support what they had done. In fact, the American president Dwight Eisenhower was openly critical of Britain and France. Nasser's stand against two major European powers brought him huge popularity, not just in Egypt but also in all Arab nations. After this success, Nasser set about the 'Egyptianisation' of his country.

Following British Prime Minster Sir Anthony Eden's brush with Nasser, the Egyptian blockade of the Suez waterway had many upsetting consequences, including the implementation of petrol rationing in the UK. In Dublin, on November 30, there was the announcement the Republic of Ireland would introduce petrol rationing on January 1, 1957.

Team arriving in Melbourne 1956

Maeve was almost caught up in a slow-boat crisis, because marooned in the middle of the Canal was the Ireland ladies' hockey team. The irony of her selection to the Irish Olympic team was that she turned down a trip on the high seas to Australia with the international hockey squad.

For Maeve, six months away from her family would have been too much - and, of course, her selection for the Melbourne Olympics changed her sporting priorities.

Ironically, the liner with the Irish hockey team on board became stuck in the Suez Canal during the Egyptian government's blockade.

However, the Ballymena athlete had her own crisis to contend with on the journey home from Melbourne.

Ronnie Delany had an uneasy feeling from the moment the aeroplane made a shuddering lift-off in Sydney. Ireland's golden wonder at Melbourne felt the Pan-American Clipper aircraft was overly loaded to the gills with passengers and baggage.

"This flight was a terrifying experience," recalls Ronnie. "I was sitting beside Maeve on the take-off from Sydney. The aircraft seemed for a moment unable to get into the air. The two us felt that maybe we were heading to our doom, because the aeroplane required such a long time to achieve lift-off. We obviously shared this experience, and immediately afterwards agreed our lives flashed before us. Flying in those days was so arduous. On that journey home across the Pacific we had a tremendously nerve-wrecking incident at Canton, when the plane suffered engine failure.

The basic thing was that aircraft at that time could have an engine fault, so you would shut that engine down. Then you would stop somewhere en-route for repairs. Everywhere we went we seemed to have an engine failure. You were terrified of flying, and the journeys took so long."

Past exploits apparently have a habit of flashing through the brain cells when the future suddenly seems totally uncertain, and likely to blank out. Delany was right in the eye of an anxiety crisis in December 1956. The petrified passengers faced that horrific predicament, staring death in the face.

Maeve and most members of Ireland's team were involved in the pulse-racing predicament.

The cream of Irish athletic talent, including some of the world's best boxers, was on board the fraught flight when some of the aeroplane's engines caught fire. The passengers were reduced to total silence during a white-knuckle nightmare. Everything seemed to take on time-warp proportion. Maeve recalled one of the most hellishly frightening happenings of her much-travelled life. She reluctantly relived the trouble at 35,000 feet, when it became a case of panic over the Pacific Ocean.

"One of my next-seat passengers was a boxer who tugged at my sleeve, when I was having a doze, to point out through a window. I didn't like what I saw. There were sparks coming out of an engine. Oh, I was told - take a look out again, because it was the same thing with another engine," she recalls.

"Oh my God. What am I doing here? My lovely daughter Shauna and my husband Sean are back in Ballymena. I might never see them again. Here I am, frightened out of my wits, in an aeroplane I felt could crash into the sea at any moment. We were certainly in deep problems.

We asked the stewardess why this was, and soon we were told the news we dreaded, confirmation there was a growing major technical problem. We feared the worst, and were told we would have to make an emergency landing on Canton Island. The next thing was, the air stewardesses came down the plane, and gave us instructions on what to do if we had to get out in the water from a crash landing.

It was as serious as that. The little boxer had his head down, and his rosary beads out.

My mind was drifting in all directions, convinced we would finish up in the water, and that a barracuda would get me. I had this daft notion I might arrive home with one leg missing, if I was lucky. Mercifully, we landed safely at Canton, which was an atoll made into an air base during the War. The plane slipped down there with the wings over the water, because the runway was so small.

An Irish couple looked after tourists on the island, a base shared by the Americans and the British during the War. Aeroplanes had to stop off there for refuelling. There was damn all at the place. A coral atoll - that was it. We had to stay there for quite a while, to complete repairs. It was turning into an adventure like that of Indiana Jones."

Belfast boxer Freddie Gilroy retraced the terror trail.

"One of the engines caught fire. It started to spread, and another engine caught fire. It flared up again, and everybody started to panic. The pilot advised us not to be alarmed, not to worry, 'take it easy, I'm knocking the other engines off', he said. There were two engines in each wing. Anyway, the pilot started cutting out the engines, and also telling us we were about to float down for repairs. We started singing to keep spirits up.

The pilot was terrific, taking the plane down successfully. That was really something, and with so many lives at stake. He guided the plane down, floated it like a butterfly - otherwise we might not be here today to tell the tale.

Later, we stopped off at Honolulu with some seven hours to kill but as we walked into the airport, there was a call for us over the intercom - for the Irish Olympic team members to go to the foyer. Waiting for us there was famous film actor Ward Bond and film producer John Ford. They heard we were there, and because we had a few hours to spend before the next flight, they volunteered to show us around."

Maeve added: "Travelling was quite exhausting. Still, we had no real problems flying out to the Games. When we stopped at Fiji, landing at six o'clock in the morning, we had a pineapple breakfast - given to us by the Friendly Brothers of St Patrick. They were descendants of Irish folk living there. People were so kind, and on the way back we stopped off at Honolulu where John Ford entertained us. That was a great thrill, being feted by John Ford."

Maeve's elation at the stardust setting of the Olympic Games in Melbourne disappeared just as quickly into a mental tailspin when son Michael John tragically died shortly after birth, in 1957. That was a heartbreaking period for the Kyle family.

84

The resilient Mrs Kyle, however, proved to be made of remarkably strong stuff, overcoming the tragedy with a steely dignity - always comforted by the quiet reassuring strength of Sean. The combined family faith helped to overcome this terrible dark time.

"That's life," shrugged Maeve, understandably uneasy when discussing this unfortunate event in her life.

"We lost our second child, a boy. He was three months old, gorgeous - but he had a heart problem. Part of the outside heart muscle was missing. It was hard, a great pity. We took Michael John to the City Hospital to see Dr Muriel Fraser. Nothing could be done."

The Kyle family tragedy held wider implications, as Maeve explains:

"The death of Michael John was sad in a whole lot of ways. There are no boys in Sean's side of the family. There are no Kyle boys, but there are Shankey boys. Sean's brother had two daughters in his family."

With typical determination, Maeve quickly sought and secured a certain degree of solace in something she knew best - sport.

"I found the most rewarding way to try to face up to and overcome the very sad setback was to concentrate on my athletics, my training, I was also helped by my little daughter Shauna.

Another factor, later on in September 1958, that helped take me through the trauma was that I returned to teaching."

John Ford

85

Cardiff Capers

Maeve joined the staff at Cambridge House in Ballymena, where she taught science subjects. At that time, the School was on the Ballymoney Road. There, she also helped to create an interest in athletics, and soon had the school competing in championships.

Miss Patricia Owens was the Head of Cambridge House at the time and she had very broad ideas on what education should be about. Maeve helped coach at the school and she was also back training regularly. From that old school playground Maeve managed to produce a team of top-class girls to win the All-Ireland Schools' Championship.

"That was something else," said Maeve. "Our daughter Shauna was in that team. She was around 13 years of age at the time, and later became an international hurdler. I tried to introduce kids to a sport that was individual. Not everyone wants to play team games. I offered them something they could do on their own. They were responsible for the outcome, if you like."

That little acorn of interest set by Maeve was bearing fruit at Cambridge House, something that would prove to be the cornerstone to her unstinting interest in coaching at Ballymena and Antrim AC. Then, there was her significant breakthrough to represent Northern Ireland in the first of two occasions at the

Maeve - Opening Twickenham Track, London

Commonwealth Games. Her debut was at the last staging of the old Empire Games, at Cardiff in 1958.

Maeve's mum and dad travelled to Wales, to look after Shauna, Sean was team coach, initially, and then became team manager. The Northern Ireland team included boxer Terry Milligan, who was the sole gold medal winner, while the

Maeve at Cherryvale in Belfast

other boxing medallists were Jim Jordan, with a silver - and bronze medallists by Peter Lavery, Dickie Hanna and John McClory.

Paddy Toner, once a cigar-chewing sports journalist and quality sprinter, also competed at Cardiff. He remembers, with great affection, Maeve's class on the track.

"Maeve blazed a trail in women's athletics, one that culminated in Mary Peters lifting gold at the Olympics at Munich in 1972," he said.

Maeve - Tokyo

"She was an amazing girl, an all-round athlete, competing in the 110 and 220 yards. Maeve's husband Sean coached Ronnie Chambers, Gordon Hamilton, Peter Street and myself for the 4 x 110 yards at Cardiff."

The Northern Ireland women's 4 x 110 relay team of high jumper Thelma Hopkins, javelin thrower Brigid Robinson, all-rounder Mary Peters and Maeve reached the final.

"We qualified, but England's team broke the world record in the final. When the last English girl was on her way with the baton I was standing on the side of the

89

Mary Peters, Jean Hood, Maeve Kyle, Marjorie Bell & Shauna

Maeve at Santry, Dublin after a thunderstorm

lane waiting for Mary (Peters) to come round the bend with our baton. We finished last. It didn't matter. Importantly, it was a breakthrough for Northern Ireland, a first time for a ladies team to reach the final.

Don't forget, women's athletics in Northern Ireland was in the very early stage of development," said Maeve.

The Empire Games also created another interesting milestone in Northern Ireland sport. It was to mark the beginnings of devoted service by very capable legislator Dick McColgan. Cardiff also had a special meaning for Sean Kyle and the link to Dick McColgan.

It was to be the dawn of another new era.

Sean went to the Empire Games as a Technical Official, representing Northern Ireland in the athletics. However circumstances started to change around a week before the Games when Team Manager Tommy Ferguson was rushed to hospital with a suspected heart attack.

Captain T D Morrison was Chief of the team, sent for Sean and asked him if he would come on board as Team Manager and coach.

Sean had already checked in with the Games officials as a Technical Officer, and he went back the next morning to inform them he had been appointed as Team Manager. The Northern Ireland team still required someone to take over from Sean at the athletics - and he recommended Dick McColgan.

"I had my car over at Cardiff, got into it - and eventually found Dick, who came in and took my place as Technical Official," said Sean.

"During the Games, Captain Morrison suggested to me in The Village we should have a proper Northern Ireland Association. He remarked it was ridiculous sending people to the Games and not having a Northern Ireland Federation. I said, fair enough.

He added that we needed someone in Belfast to develop the thing, and I suggested there was a very good young fellow down below at the Games - Dick McColgan."

Rome and Tokyo

Maeve's good times on cross-channel tracks led to her second appearance in the Olympic Games, this time in 1960, and a first visit to Rome. She represented Ireland in the 100 and 200 metres at the Games that would launch Cassius Clay on the path to boxing and worldwide stardom.

The Rome Olympics proved to be an entirely different experience from the adventure in Melbourne four years earlier, with Sean close by, staying in the heart of Rome.

Maeve setting new Irish 800m record 1964

Joe Riverson, Maeve, Jimmy Ogabemi, Joan Atkinson and a Yale athlete - Belfast 1963

Irish Team V Belgium - Maeve was Irish Captain
First Irish Men's and Women's Team

"I made a couple of trips from the Olympic Village into Rome to see Sean. He was staying in rented accommodation, in the house Prince Charlie was born in, right in the middle of the city," remembers Maeve.

"The house had a plaque on it, and you went in through a courtyard that included chickens and washing, and then into the most beautiful apartment, via a bird-cage lift. The 1960 Olympics are often referred to as the birth of legendary American boxer Cassius Clay. You couldn't help but notice this young man.

Even back then you felt he was something special. I recall Cassius Clay walking round the Olympic Village with the gold medal around his neck, so proud. Clay was brash, but with that glorious innocence. He was on top of the world."

Maeve's exploits though were of a much humbler level than Clay's, as she failed to qualify out of her first round heats in both the 110 and 220 yards.

"I had the greatest knack of drawing the world champion or the world record holder in the heats at major athletic meetings," she said.

"I was absolutely expert at that, and also drawing the outside lane. The big thing to come out of Rome was the International Federation's decision to include

93

Breaking World Indoor 400m Record, Wembley, 1962

competition at 400 and 800 metres in the next Olympics, the 1964 Games at Tokyo. That intrigued me, and on the way home from Italy I discussed it with Sean. I told him I would like to try the 400 metres, try for a place in Tokyo 1964.

Just shows you how silly I was. When I ran in Rome I was 32 years of age. Here was I talking about the next Olympic Games when I'd be 36...complete madness.

I was running against young girls, yet the 400 kept me interested. I was intrigued. It was a new challenge for me, I felt. I had to accept I was never going to be a world-class sprinter, so I had nothing to lose. I might as well try this new event. I was in great shape, still playing away at hockey. So, I decided I would train for the 400 metres, a ladies event that featured in the European Championships since the late Fifties."

Maeve started running the 400 metres shortly after the Rome Olympics, and was never beaten in Northern Ireland, at 400. She was, and is, fortunate enough to be married to a man who thinks middle-distance running is God's gift to world athletics! Sean wanted Maeve to run the 800 metres, but her love of the 400 where, in her own lane, her own territory she could decide how to run her races rather than the pushing and shoving that could go on in the 800 metres was the deciding factor.

Maeve won the British 400 metres title in 1961, setting a new British record time of 56.3 secs at White City and becoming the first Irish female to triumph in the British track championships.

Lorna McGarvey beats the Middlesex 100m Champion
Ballymena Showgrounds

Lord Burley awards Maeve 400m Medal - World Record 1962

In 1964, when retaining the Scottish 400 metres title at Ayr, Maeve clocked a time of 55.7 seconds, the ninth fastest time in the world over 400 metres.

She celebrated her 36th birthday on October 6, 1964, on the day she arrived with the Ireland team in Tokyo.

At the 1964 Games, Maeve reached both the semi-finals of the 400 and 800 metres, but by her own admittance she could, and should, have done better

Wembley 400m Indoors, 1962

Maeve winning 80m Hurdles, Shorts AC Belfast, 1963

Olympic 800m Semi-final - Tokyo 1964

Maeve winning 400m indoors

"I should have been in both the 400 and 800 finals. I was running very well that summer, and defeated most of the girls who were in Japan for the Games - but I had to qualify too often," she said. "It didn't happen for me. I thought it was time to quit, yet in 1966 I went to the European Championships in Dortmund against my better judgement."

99

At the Europeans Maeve ran impressively in the 400 metres, clocking 57.3, finishing behind ace Helga Henning, who was timed at 56.9.

However, that same year, 1966, there was no Commonwealth Games team recognition.

"I was overlooked for the Northern Ireland team at Jamaica, where the great boxer Jim McCourt took home gold. My best friend Lorna McGarvey, my training companion, went and also Johnny Kilpatrick, a very good sprinter that Sean was coaching," Maeve said.

"Then it was 1968, and the Olympic Games in Mexico. I was asked to train for that, but said no.

I would not go because it was at altitude - and I did not know how I would react. In retrospect, it was a wise decision, considering my potential, but unknown then, heart problem. It could have been quite serious. Sean went to Mexico on his own but we had a colour television in then, and I was able to watch it. At that time I was still playing hockey, but around 1968 I played my last international."

100

Family Matters

Shauna Kyle concedes she did not like being involved in athletics, yet was born into the sport and progressed to international status as a quality hurdler.

"I did not particularly like athletics," she admits. "I just didn't enjoy it, yet it was what I grew up with. I was virtually reared on running tracks. There is a photograph of me as a toddler playing with starting blocks. I suppose athletics came automatically really. You just did it. I became a hurdler, an Irish champion and Irish record holder for a long time at 80 metres and 100 metres. However, I didn't really do an awful lot of athletics when I was at university in England.

Some time after I came back from Birmingham I returned to athletics, when I was 27 - and did one season. I had injuries and setbacks. Still, I was back on the Northern Ireland team during that one season, as a 100 metres hurdler. I said then, I'd had enough - that was it. I coached for a while after that, and also played a bit of social hockey.

I was never really involved in the athletics crowd. It was just one of those things. Mummy was too well known, so I did my own thing, really. Mummy was still running at top level when I was competing, and we were in the same international relay team. It is always a bit difficult if you have a famous parent when trying to fit into the groove. I was good at athletics, and I am very proud of my parents and their involvement in athletics - and also the achievements of Ballymena and

101

Sean, Maeve and Shauna

Antrim Athletic Club - but the one sport I preferred, of all the sports I was involved in, was hockey. I played a lot of hockey while at university. I played for the English Universities. Before that, I played at Ulster Schools level and later Senior League with Instonians."

Shauna has always been involved in drama and is a graduate in drama from Birmingham University. Her career as a Thespian moved recently back to acting with Theatre Three at Newtownabbey.

"I wanted to go to RADA [Royal Academy for Dramatic Art], so I went to a university where I could read drama," she said.

"I came back to Northern Ireland in 1978. I was a 1977 Drama and English graduate. Again, I became involved in drama, which started with the Lyric Youth Theatre, all through my teens. I did a lot of school's broadcasting and stuff like that. Drama was my great love, and still is. I am with Theatre Three, and acting again, what I really like to do.

Maeve and Sean at RDS, Dublin, 1953

Before that, I also was involved in a couple of plays at Cushendall, as a producer for the Lurig Drama Society. I did that because there was nobody else, at the time. I much prefer being involved in acting. I produced one play - "Remembrance", for the Slemish Drama Group, reaching the Ulster finals. Fergus Boyle also won the Best Young Actor award. One of two plays produced for Lurig - "Poker Session", also reached the Ulster finals."

Since her return from Birmingham University, Shauna has been in the family business, Kyle Insurance Brokers. She did not intend to be involved with the firm in Ballymena.

"My father suggested I pay off my university overdraft by working in the office. I have been there ever since. I suppose as a drama graduate there wasn't an awful lot else for me in those days so I settled into the business, did my professional

105

Ballymena Showgrounds, 1960

Paddy, Maeves training partner
106

Sean, Maeve, Shauna and Paddy, 1964

examinations, and was the first woman in the UK to be a regional chairman of the professional body - the British Insurance Brokers' Association (BIBA), and also serve on the Belfast Chartered Insurance Institute Council."

In Autumn 2005, Shauna re-opened an old family link with Alexandra College. Her daughter, Indy became a boarder at the Dublin centre of education, where there are 600 girl students, including 140 boarders. Born in April 1993, Indy is named after her great-grandmother, Enid Shankey, as Shauna explains: "The name Indy doesn't stand for anything, it was my grandmother's pet name! Mummy's mother was Enid Thrift, but couldn't say the word Enid when she was a child - and called herself Indy. That name stuck with her, even when she went to university.

My Indy absolutely loves school at Alexandra College. She is a very independent young lady, and is quite a promising hurdler but we don't push it at all. It will happen if it happens."

Maeve & Shauna training

Shauna, Irish Schools 80m Champion, 1972

Difficult Hurdles

Sean and Maeve have in-built stubborn streaks, a strict code of fair play, and repeatedly refused to knuckle under to what were perceived unfair obstacles placed in their paths.

Some hurdles for Maeve away from the track were more difficult to surmount than others. Her first brush with what was viewed as archaic overview on the then limited role by females in athletics, was in the Republic during her opening interest in track competition.

Women's athletics became handcuffed to prudish ideals, proving a powerful challenge for Maeve. She became a suffragette for the sport and opened eyes and minds during an early part of her sporting life. It was a time when there was that overly rigid concern in the Republic of Ireland about modesty - in not allowing females to participate in athletics and cycling.

In 1947, Crusaders formed a ladies' section in the progressive Dublin athletic club, and held a first meeting a year later at Lansdowne Road. Maeve ran in the sprint.

But, in 1950, Dr John Charles McQuaid, the Archbishop of Dublin, issued a Lental Pastoral that objected to females competing in athletics, unless adhering to a code of dress. A year later the ladies' section at Crusaders was disbanded.

109

Sean, Maeve and Paddy, Ballymena Showgrounds, 1960

Women participating in athletic sports had to abide by the dress code, although Maeve felt the dictate issued by Archbishop McQuaid was largely misinterpreted at the time. New dress was needed, as people wearing shorts were objected to, and there were folk who became quite uptight about this issue.

"Women in society in Ireland, at that time, were very much second-class citizens," recounts Maeve. "Married women did not work then, it was felt their true place was in the home. It was a different outlook in that age than we have today. Times of enlightenment were just around the corner, I felt. I ran 100 yards at the start - when I was around 19 years of age, and in a meeting at Lansdowne Road. I did not do athletics again, until I met Sean in 1953. I was reaching 25 years of age then."

Her successes did, in turn, revive interest in ladies' athletics in the South during the early Sixties. Her old club, Crusaders re-launched the ladies' section in 1962. Throughout all the eye-catching exploits, the free-spirited Maeve also had to endure some barbed comments, mysterious blockades, and also occasional insidious attempts to prevent her progress. She remains an open book on the subject, and is adamant there was more misunderstanding than real bias towards her throughout her sporting career.

110

Commonwealth Games Team, Edinburgh, 1970

"I never felt there was any bias towards me. I certainly was unaware of it if there was any. Way back in the early days, when not given credit or recognition, we hadn't all grown up in those times as a country," she said.

"I felt the South was always very much on the defensive. Sean batted for me. He does not hold grudges, but remembers things he did not like. I couldn't be bothered getting into any of that. I always felt people had a certain specific reason for saying what they said, or doing what they did. It has been claimed I said things off the top of my head, not thinking them through. That is totally untrue. I always think everything through before I speak. I may have the thing flying around and around in my head for days before that.

"Equally, and it was the way I was reared, I always believed people need to know what things were said and why things were done - and it is always possible other people made decisions or said things completely off the top of their heads. You need to know why they did it. You try to figure out the mindset. I recall one article in a Dublin daily paper, leading up to the 1956 Olympics, stating it was an absolute scandal this young married women - me, was going to run international races - and leave husband and family to do so! All that did, was to give a reflection of society at the time. Before that, married women did not work. It was felt a married woman's place was in the home - in the kitchen - full stop, end of story. But, things

111

N.I. Women's Team, Commonwealth Games, Edinburgh, 1970

were changing. Females like me were beginning to emerge and compete on a regular basis. Looking back on it, I am quite certain there were people who felt this was the way to show we were moving forward."

Sean has his own erudite view on Maeve's varied setbacks: "Through sport I believe you get a reflection of the political situation at a particular time in a country. The two things run in juxtaposition. Maeve and I would not have been, in the Northern Ireland situation, considered flavour of the month. This is largely because we would look at an All-Ireland situation. If a fellow plays rugby for All Ireland, or a girl swims for All Ireland, or a player plays hockey for all Ireland, or a boxer boxes for all Ireland, then why not athletics?

The main sports divided are athletics, soccer and cycling. The latter sport seems to be unifying ideas. Cycling has been up and down and round the corner half-a-dozen times. It is my contention Maeve should have competed in four, not two Commonwealth Games for Northern Ireland. She made her debut in the last Empire Games, at Cardiff 1958. She should, in my view, have been at Perth, Western Australia, in 1962, and Jamaica in 1966.

"The irony was, she was called back in 1970 - to make up a relay team at Edinburgh. At 42 years of age, she was a proud double finalist for Northern

Ireland, with the relay team, and also made the final of the 400 metres. I remain convinced she could have won medals in '62 and '66. The girl who took the silver medal at 400 metres was Deirdre Watkinson. Before the Games, Maeve never ever lost to her when they competed at other meetings. Maeve defeated this girl half-a-dozen times on the trot."

Sean can exude a prickly side to his nature, and understandably so when it comes to any degree of snub against Maeve, even all those years ago. It still rankles a little bit. The Kyles have been at the coalface of athletics since the early 1950's. In those days, local athletics was run by the NIAAA [Northern Ireland Amateur Athletic Association], for men, and the NIWAAA [Northern Ireland Women's Amateur Athletic Association] for females. Then it combined to become the NIAF [Northern Ireland Athletic Federation] in the early 1990's.

Maeve Kyle was the first NIAF President, the first Patron was Mary Peters and the first Chairperson was Adrienne Smyth. All three were Ballymena and Antrim club athletes, and coached at one time or other by Sean Kyle.

However, for the World Cross Country Championships in Belfast in 2001 there was a sudden change at the top table. It was felt by the men's association that it would not be a good idea to have women greeting World officials coming into Northern Ireland for the Championships, so the President was changed.

"Here we had a situation with Maeve, a highly articulate and educated woman, given the elbow before the big occasion," Sean claims. "There was one vote in it, to get her out. Maeve spent thousands upon thousands of pounds of her own money to help further the interests of athletics in Northern Ireland, and hundreds of thousands of hours of her own time to promote the sport, yet has been on the receiving end of some peculiar decisions.

Perhaps some people would like to airbrush out the efforts and contributions of the Kyle family, and the Ballymena and Antrim A.C. In my own case, some achievements have been conveniently overlooked, I feel. I was the first ever Track and Field referee for Northern Ireland, doing the job not once but twice at the Commonwealth Games. Such facts seem to be bypassed nowadays, as it was recently claimed in a Sunday newspaper column that somebody else was the first championship Track and Field referee. Perhaps NIA Federation people think so. I was also elected as Northern Ireland Coach of the Year. Later I became the UK Coach of the Year in 1987.

"Some seven years later, another NI Coach of the Year was forwarded for the Great Britain Coach of the Year. He didn't get it. Sports Council officials were in touch with me about something else, and mentioned this. They were putting out information that this was Northern Ireland's first Coach of the Year. I explained to them this was not the case. They would not even accept my word, and to prove the point I had to send them copies of cuttings and photographs out of The Times

- showing when not only was I a first NI Coach of the Year - but was the GB Coach as well. Such oversights can be a frustration, but you have to get on and get over such irritations."

Maeve also experienced the old adage "not a prophet in her own land" when it came to using her global hockey experiences for coaching advice at local level. The Canadians recognised her worth and she did a stint of successful tutoring in Quebec during the mid-Seventies. She was coach to the Ulster Junior Women's Squad for one season, winning the Inter-Provincial championship, but before the final game Maeve was told there was no need for her to travel to a southern venue with the team. She was never asked to coach after that.

Bumpy Begginings

In 1953, Maeve made her first impression on the Northern Ireland athletics scene at Celtic Park on the Donegall Road, home of the famous but long since defunct Belfast Celtic soccer team.

Maeve had been running well, beating the so-called professional athletes such as Pat Kennedy. She had already won at Ravenhill and was dubbed ' Blonde Bombshell' in the press!

At the Northern Ireland Women's championships at Celtic Park, Maeve won the 110 and 220 yards but the officials wouldn't award her the medals claiming she wasn't eligible. That was the start of her 'interesting' relationship with the Northern Ireland authorities in the sport.

"I am not a confrontational sort of person, really - but I have this inbuilt sense of justice - and, at times, that doesn't go down well," admits Maeve.

"Perhaps one of the reasons then was because I was still playing hockey for Leinster. I also felt a lot of people made instant decisions about me - because I was from the South. There was the automatic assumption I must be Catholic, and I therefore I'd have to be a Nationalist. At times like those, when prejudices were around, I thought of who I was.

My Father was in the Masonic Order. My grandfather was a great churchman, and was high up in the Masons. I was brought up to say my prayers in any church. The Lord isn't bothered, I feel, so long as you say them. That was the way I was. I found this opposition to me very, very strange and foreign to my upbringing. When Sean and I were married, here was I coming up from the South to this Presbyterian house in Ballymena. The Kyle family were strong yet liberal Presbyterians. A lot of their friends must have thought I was Catholic, yet I belonged to a strong Protestant family in a strong Catholic area in County

114

Thelma Hopkins, 1956

Kilkenny. Northern Ireland has changed so much, and so quickly, since I first came to Ballymena."

After the medals incident at Celtic Park, Maeve continued to attract attention. There was very good press coverage of athletics in those days, and her name was ever prominent. People were looking for an outlet to put running into a slightly

115

different perspective, to escape from bias - as opposed to the strictures on female athletes in the South.

Ladies' athletics in Northern Ireland was enjoying a flourishing formative period. The first NI Women's Championships were held in 1949, and Dutch coach Franz Stampfl was hired to help promote the sport. Out of that emerged such outstanding talents as Thelma Hopkins, who excelled at hockey, high and long jump. Miss Hopkins competed at 16 years of age in the 1952 Olympic Games in Helsinki 1952 for Great Britain, and finished fourth in the high jump.

When Maeve married Sean, and moved to Ballymena, she competed regularly in Northern Ireland sprint events. Amongst her many successes, she won the 400 metres title from 1959 right through 1970.

In 1959, she was timed at 60.0 seconds, trimmed the time to 57.7 in 1960, lowered it to 56.9 in 1962, to 56.6 in 1964, and astonishingly in her 1970 swansong appearance over this distance, clocked a farewell 56.4 seconds.

After being repeatedly ignored and overlooked during her prime, it seemed somewhat incongruous Maeve was selected to rejoin the Northern Ireland team for the 1970 Commonwealth Games in Edinburgh - her first selection since Cardiff in 1958.

It was a bolt from the blue, because the then Ballymena teacher and housewife was 41 years of age!

Still remarkably fit, Maeve continued to be active on the domestic track, nonetheless.

"I always kept myself fairly fit throughout my career. Alongside the athletics, I continued to play serious hockey," she said.

"Around 1968, I played my last international. I also quit competitive athletics after the 1970 Commonwealth Games at Meadowbank, Edinburgh. It is a fact I was not remotely connected to the Games situation in the first place, and had not been selected since Cardiff 1958.

But at that time, 1970, Sean had a 4x100 relay team that was short a runner. I was just doing club athletics. I wasn't being serious. 'Don't look at me, I told him'. He needed a fourth girl. He had Noleen McGarvey and Adrienne Smyth from the Ballymena club, both coached by Sean - and Linda Teskey, a very good club sprinter from Belfast Ladies. I normally trained with them.

I went to the NI championships that summer, at the Queen's University track. Sean entered me, not only in the 100m but also in the 400m. I have to be honest.

Maeve, Sir Menzies Campbell and Shauna, 1963

Before that, I agreed to go in the relay, but I knew from personal pride I needed to do well in the domestic championships.

I ran and won the 400m title, and was selected for the Commonwealth Games in that discipline, and also for the relay team. If I didn't go in the relay the other girls could not be sent. So we went to Edinburgh, and would you believe it the 4x100m team reached the final. In the 400m, I also reached the final. Those Games, I recall, proved not to be a pleasant experience, because they were staged in the most disgustingly wet weather."

Shortly after coming home from Edinburgh, Maeve celebrated her 42nd birthday. It was time, she felt, to bring to an end her days of competitive athletics.

While her running days may have been over, Maeve was about to embark on a supremely satisfying and fruitful time as a specialist coach with Ballymena and Antrim AC.

Off And Running

Ballymena AC was originally a ladies' club. The inaugural members were mostly girls out of the Mid-Antrim Hockey Club, who wanted to train and be fully fit for the September start to the hockey season and that was the basis on which athletics gained the first foothold in the Ballymena area, in 1954.

In 1955, Roy Bonnar first had the idea along with Alex Campbell - a schoolteacher at Ballymena Academy, of forming a boys' athletic club. They also launched a men's club some eight months later and the logical thing then was that the two organisations, male and female, should get together. Manifesting out of that emerged the Ballymena Athletic Club and later what is the present Ballymena and Antrim Athletic Club.

In those days the men wore black and white, the same as the Ballymena Rugby Club colours, and the girls wore green and white. Black, green and white remain the club colours today.

Barry Bamber was one of the club's first main male athletes, a hurdler and high jumper. Also, there was discus thrower Evan McKinney, of J H McKinney and Sons - the auctioneers, along with Jimmy Penny and Des O'Kane, who ran the 800 metres. The Club had a sound basis, good numbers, and solid members with excellent ability to start with.

Club Team, 1962

In the ladies' section, there were such talents as sprinters Marjorie Bell, Maeve Kyle, Catherine McCurdy, high jumper Jean Hood, Marjorie Hood - a sprinter, and Deirdre Dinsmore [Carson].

With over 50 years of unparalleled dedication to athletics, it continues to be a totally rewarding experience for the Kyles.

"It has been all very worthwhile, and still is. It is our life," said Maeve.

"For a kid to achieve his or her particular goal, even to make the school final or make the school team - or whatever, that in itself is an achievement. It is a joy to watch the delight on the faces of the youngsters.

Less than 10 years ago, we had to have a vision - and a mission, suggested by a Sports Council scheme. Two things came out of it. We had a general meeting at the Club, and we asked the kids who should be running the club, and they said - the adults.

So we asked them 'who tells those people what they want?' The answer from the kids was that 'it has to be the athletes'.

The 'Originals' - Catherine McCurdy, Mary Peters, Deirdre Dinsmore and Maeve

Ballymena and Antrim AC is the lone club where the only people who have a vote are the athletes of any age, those who are fully paid up members - and who have competed within the previous twelve months. That is great. It is democracy at work.

We can come and help out in disputes, and offer suggestions, but ultimately the kids then make the decisions. One interesting thing emerged from that. At one AGM, they voted to go out of all leagues. Sean and I said; 'wait a minute, hold on, let's think this one through.' We asked. 'Where are you going to compete?'

The athletes felt, after looking at the programme, there was plenty of other competition. They said they didn't like having to compete in events in which they hadn't been trained for - and in disciplines they didn't want to do.

We suggested to them 'surely you are doing it for the Club, to get points for the Club'. They replied. 'We are the Club'.

We asked the kids. 'What is the Club, what do you want out of the Club, in which direction should the Club be going?' They came back with what I think is a most marvellous visionary statement; 'The Club is a safe place where we can go, and where we can be coached to do the best we can in our events, to go as far as we can go in our events, and as far as we want to go.'

120

Club Team, Eaton Park, Ballymena, 1959

Our Club, which presently has around 100 active athletes, suddenly changed from being totally coach-led to being athlete centred and driven. This is good."

Ballymena and Antrim AC has approximately a 50 percent divide between male and female members, with perhaps 20 percent over the age of 21. There are big numbers in the middle-age section, which is the 13 to 18 age group, and amongst the senior ranks are internationals Paul Brizel, Anna Boyle, Nigel Carlisle, Gareth Hill and Zoë Brown.

However, as Maeve acknowledges, most of the kids in the last 30 years, who came out of college and invariably moved to Universities found it hard to maintain interest in the structured training for athletics and it was, and is, hard to keep them.

"Sadly, a terrific number of kids in country areas who win at cross-country then leave the district at 16, go out of Parish and club control and are gone from the sport," said Maeve.

"We feel Ballymena and Antrim AC has a good identity, and it is a totally neutral club, in a totally neutral area. Parents are happy to send their kids to our Club, because it is in a safe environment. Our facilities are grand. We have a Clubroom, and it is adequate.

Club Team, Showgrounds, 1962

We were recently asked to do a template on the structure of our club for Irish Athletics. It was basically looking at how clubs were run. We were asked, as one of the medium-sized clubs in the country, what makes us successful? We don't know about that - never really thought of it that way - but, this is the way we operate. We operate as a small business. It is long past the day when you can run athletics as an amateur sport, through the use of volunteers - on an amateur basis.

We discussed how we could and should run the club and make plans for the future. The athletes came back, and said they wanted five managers. The managers have no vote. As a coach you start with the 16 year olds. The youngsters are asked to take some responsibility for the outcome of their own actions. Later on, they are asked to take on more responsibility. We have tried to develop responsible adults, whether they become good athletes or not is almost secondary. We have very, very good people at our club, and mixed in every sense of the word. Mixed in every way you could think of - in creed, colour, and in class. It is their club, their family, and that is where they are comfortable."

Maeve and Sean are the first to admit the Club's success over the last 50 years hasn't all been down to them.

Maeve beating Noleen McGarvey, Ravenhill, 1969

Hilary Brady and the late Des Allen are regarded as serious influential contributors to the relentless rise of Ballymena AC, and there were many people down the past five decades who made an impact in helping the Club become an institution in the area, and the tentacles gradually spread throughout Irish and UK athletics.

123

Club Group, 1979

Maeve suggests the original baton carriers, to create a stable situation for school kids to test their ability in athletics, were Des Allen and Hilary Brady.

"They were then PE teachers at Ballymena Academy and were enormously influential in athletics in the Town," she said.

"We had a ready-made nursery of budding athletes, children introduced to the various sports at the Academy. The late Dessie Allen, who has a Suite named after him at Ballymena Showgrounds, left teaching and entered Local Authority to become the chief officer for Leisure in Ballymena. When I was teaching in Cambridge House, there was a girls' athletic association - and a schoolboys' athletic association.

Heather Neeson, from Victoria College, Jim Shaw, from Coleraine Inst. and myself managed to put together a structure for a Federation for School's athletics in Ulster. The kids had their Sports Day at the Academy, and from that most of the youngsters came into the Ballymena AC. We had some of the most fabulous kids progress from that early introduction and grooming in sport including Johnny Kilpatrick, who went on to become a Great Britain international. He ran in 100 metres and the 200 metres at the 1966 Commonwealth Games in Jamaica, and also at the 1970 Games in Edinburgh. Billy McCue went to the Commonwealth Games as well."

40th Anniversary of Club
Kath Hounslow   Deirdre Carson   Sheena Golding   Marjorie McDowell
(Nee McCurdy)   (Nee Dinsmore)   (Nee Donaghy)   (Nee Bell)

Sean was the one and only coach, when the Ballymena Athletics Club was formed. He was also Secretary and Treasurer, while James Sampson was Chairman.

"It is, I accept," said Sean, "very hard for modern-day people to understand a club having merely one coach for everything. Nowadays, there is a different type of coach available for various disciplines."

Antrim was incorporated into the name in 1981, as Maeve explained: "When we went to Antrim, we had to be Ballymena and Antrim AC, and the Antrim side of this really started in 1981. The track at Antrim Forum opened in 1980. We first went there in 1979, to work on the base of the track. It was the first leisure centre in Northern Ireland, and opened in the early 1970's.

We were fortunate there to have an almost endless assembly line of quality athletes - we had the Kirkpatrick brothers, CJ and Billy. CJ became one of the best hurdlers Great Britain ever had, and Billy was one of the most accomplished long jumpers Great Britain ever had.

We also had other excellent athletes, such as Mark Forsythe and Ricky Robinson from Ballyclare High. Ballymena and Antrim AC also enjoyed a big influx of

125

Club Team, Mary Peters Track, Belfast

burgeoning talents from Ballymena Academy, such as Mark Kirk and Angela Kirkpatrick.

Also, we had the likes of Sean O'Neill from St Louis. Incidentally, the records of Sean O'Neill and Ricky Robinson in Irish Schools' championships still stand. Sean, a brother of former Northern Ireland soccer international Michael, was an 800m specialist.

He ran in the Commonwealth Games at 18 years of age, before going to Villanova University. There was an overlap of prospects doing very well before we went to Antrim. We had people achieving top results before the switch, and so the move to Antrim proved to be very comfortable."

Fine-tuning during a demandingly exact training programme on a disused dump was hardly the most ideal or glamorous setting for a budding athlete to prepare. Still, it was one of the most popular methods in Maeve's programme during the formative days of the Ballymena Club and she recalls powering over old cinder tracks.

"I still reckon the training in that old dump was the best preparation I ever had," Maeve said.

Mary Peters

"The early AC training was at varied venues; Eaton Park, at Ballymena Showgrounds, often on the roads in the vicinity, through Portglenone Forest, and also at Ballymena Academy's grounds."

Mary Peters arrived in the second year of the Club. She had attended school at Ballymena Academy, although she was only one year there before the family moved to Portadown.

Kenny McClelland, a teacher at Portadown College, encouraged Mary to go into athletics when she was perhaps 13 or 14 years of age. Mary was an all-rounder whose father was also a very keen on sport.

Juniors - Ballymena Club, 1993

"This was around the 1956 -'57 era," said Maeve. "Mary was very friendly with Catherine McCurdy, who was at the Girls' Model School. They lived near each other.

After Mary left Ballymena, to live in Portadown, she came to us in the 15-16 age group, even though residing in Portadown.

Sean coached her up to 1962, after she was in Perth for the Commonwealth Games - where she competed in the shot. Mary was in the British team as a shot putter, and that was a tremendous achievement at that time.

She was at a Domestic College in Belfast and by then it became inconvenient to travel down to Ballymena, so she went to join the late Buster McShane. She was 22 when she left Ballymena AC, in January 1963. Before that, she had been to the Commonwealth Games, and to the Europeans, and was starting to go very well in athletics - finishing fourth in the 1962 European championships, in the Pentathlon."

The Pentathlon as an event was relatively new to Northern Ireland, being first introduced as a championship event in 1956. Sean Kyle had been at an athletics meeting in France, between the French and the Russians. Coming back in the train, he read in his fractured French the paper L'Equipe - and saw a small paragraph illustrating the winner of this new event.

It was an all-rounder tournament for women, similar to the men's decathlon but with only five events, and it was due to become an Olympic event, having been tried out in Russia and Germany.

Sean thought seriously about this innovation, and all the possibilities back home. Someone like Maeve did the 100m, the 200m, the hurdles, a bit of sprint relay and sometimes the shot. The 200m, long and high jumps, the shot putt and hurdles were the five disciplines to be introduced for women at the Olympic Games.

"I reckoned the chances of a small nation like Ireland producing anything at world level was going to be once in a lifetime - to find such a talent," said Sean.

"Against that, there is the possibility of maybe getting a person to do all five events. Therefore, the all-rounder thing held great appeal."

Sean contacted the International Association of Athletic Federations [IAAF] office, then in London, and asked for scoring tables and record forms, and any other suitable data to set the wheels in motion. The first Pentathlon championship to be held in Ireland was at Eaton Park, Ballymena, in July 1956. Sean recalled: "Great care was taken to obtain a correctly weighted shot, suitable schedules and measurement of the track. We laid out a proper high jump.

Thelma Hopkins, the former world record holder in the High Jump and a British International at Hurdles and Long Jump, was the clear winner. Maeve was second, and promising newcomer Mary Peters came third. This was Mary's introduction to the competition, one that led to Olympic Games gold - and eventually moving on to become a Dame of the British Empire."

This was arguably the true beginning of the glittering age of the golden girls with the remarkable Thelma Hopkins creating a British All-Comers record in the process. However, initially she didn't gain official recognition. Harold Abrahams, of Olympic fame, was staying at the Kyles some time later, and he took up the matter with the British Board and helped to have the record ratified. Thelma, of course, specialised in the high jump, and won silver with a jump of 1.67 metres at the 1956 Olympics, as a member of the UK team.

Before that, she sensationally recorded a then world record leap of 1.74 metres, during a meeting in Belfast's Cherryvale Park on May 5, 1956.

Gatherings at Gormanstown

Coaching at a national level had almost accidental embryonic origins when athletes from the various opposing factions unofficially gathered forces at Gormanstown College, County Meath, during Christmas 1963. The occasion

Maeve, Billy Bingham and Mary Peters training at Stranmillis

virtually laid the cornerstone thinking to a new age. The Kyles were at the coalface, with Sean the main coach.

"There was a time when you were not allowed to compete against the NACA [National Athletic & Cultural Association], if you were in the BLE [Bord Luathcleas na h-Eireann] or the AAUE [Athletic Union of Eire], or whatever, because the NACA weren't recognised by the IAAF [International Association of Athletics Federations]" said Maeve.

"There were a lot of things you could do and not do, but there was one thing the various authorities then could not stop you from doing and that was to train together. A few of us decided to get together at Gormanstown College, which had a track, a magnificent indoor sports hall, a swimming pool and a golf course.

People strongly involved in athletics then such as Iggy Moriarty, who became President of Galway University, Fergus O'Donovan of Cork, Paddy Murphy from the Bank of Ireland, and ourselves decided we would organise a training group.

Jack Sweeney, a Lecturer at UCD, was the only person to run any kind of coaching course. A couple of years before Gormanstown started, there was a summer school coaching course for people in and around the Dublin area.

130

We had a friend at Gormanstown who told us we could stay there. It was at Christmas 1963, and the College students were on vacation. We told the folk at the College there might be a maximum of 100 attending. We were not sure, as the information was through bush telegraph. On the day we arrived people kept on arriving, and arriving - 383 turned up. It was the first big coaching course gathering of its kind in Ireland.

We had the best weekend ever, and went there for years after that. We would also nip out to the Gormanstown Arms and the Cock and Hen hostelries. The evenings always ended with someone singing 'The Sash' - and somebody else singing 'The Boys from Wexford'.

It was outstanding craic, the best of times, brilliant."

Sean added: "It was decided to bring all the varied associations together. The media from Dublin came out, expecting trouble. We had unofficial competition and used teams from the Universities, a team from the Athletic Union of Ireland, and so on - four or five different teams. It worked out brilliantly. I think the AAUE team won it on that first year. There were individual prizes, and everybody was happy.

I think it created a new attitude, the first getting together of minds, really. The athletes made the decisions - the people that really matter are the athletes."

Coaching Success

Whatkeeps Sean and Maeve motivated through cold winter evenings at the club is the one athlete who they did not expect to see suddenly showing improvement on the training ground.

"You cannot wait for the moment when that athlete goes into competition," said Sean.

"That athlete will suddenly produce it in competition, and you say to yourself, 'here, I've found another one!' You will feel chuffed. By George, we've cracked it, again. You can be the greatest coach in the world, yet if athletes who want to progress and work hard have no talent they won't go to the top."

Sean's coaching has been wide and varied: He has coached discus and javelin, quite a lot of distance running, sprinting [taking in the relays] hurdling, long jump and shot. But he is one of a rare breed of coach.

Of the total number of coaches in the British Isles, approximately 1000 in athletics, around 850 are middle-distance coaches. A great deal of the rest would be sprint coaches while only around 20 are coaches specialising in the jumps and field events.

Maeve's speciality? The high jump, a discipline she sometimes feels does not get the recognition it deserves.

"What we do at the club is we try to insist the young athletes do different things, and also compete in a different event than the one they are concentrating mainly on," said Maeve.

"The kids learn how to do them properly, and also compete under no pressure. I would perhaps prefer to coach field events - high jumps and long jumps. I find

133

Sean Coaching, Ballymena Academy

sprints can be quite boring to coach, though I must confess I enjoy coaching the technical aspects of the sprints."

The insatiable quest for knowledge is never ending in the restless Kyle household, as Sean claims: "To pick up coaching knowledge, which is ever improving, you go to every seminar possible. You go to warm-weather training camps. You go to major games. You spend your time as an official and also in the warm-up area. You watch, you listen, and you talk to people. You read all you can possibly get your hands on as far as athletics is concerned.

The other thing Maeve and I would do at a major meeting is go in different directions during the tournament. We would meet up afterwards and talk things over, what we picked up.

We also have coaching friends all over the world, and we meet up at seminars, and all at our own expense."

The spectre of what seems a never-ending cycle of drug afflictions in sport worries the Kyle's. "We regularly attend seminars on the unfortunate drugs issue," Maeve said.

Maeve and Sean, 1968

"Everyone of our athletes at the Ballymena and Antrim club knows of our attitude towards drugs, that we are totally opposed to use of drugs. We encourage the athletes to come and have a chat with us, if they are puzzled or concerned about anything in this particularly thorny issue.

Mary Peters, Les Jones, Sir Brian Mawhinney and Maeve

We will give them as much information as we can. Our concern is that a youngster is not necessarily taking drugs, but a lot of them have been caught because they have taken contaminated supplements!

So, our kids do not take any supplements, unless they are approved. Sean and I have talked this over many times. What we cannot understand is why the World Anti-Doping Body cannot licence pharmaceutical companies as long as they are prepared to stand over what they are producing as being safe - and not tarnished."

Sean and Maeve's coaching achievements have been recognised by the Northern Ireland AAA, with Sean named "Coach of the Year" in 1980 and 1987, and also the UK "Coach of the Year" for all sports in 1987.

This particular high honour brought with it a very valuable scholarship that enabled the Kyles to go to Canada, and attend a major global Coaching Conference in Toronto.

Sean took his first coaching examination during the late 1950's, and between himself and Maeve they set up the first coaching structure for Northern Ireland through the Women's Association around 1961 and '62. The Men's Association would not take part in it.

136

Hilary O'Neill, from the Ulster College of Physical Education, and Katherine McTavish of Stranmillis College were great supporters of the idea of the coaching structures and they helped to set up courses for training coaches at both Stranmillis College and the Ulster College.

Sean and Maeve were both involved in delivering to athletes specific parts of the courses working through the UK qualifications.

From there, they moved on to instigate a system whereby the coaches who qualified, instead of being just attached to a club, were involved in a series held at Coaching Centres throughout Northern Ireland. The idea really took off.

It meant that if there was a high jump coach and middle distance coach in Antrim, anybody could come and be coached. It was the same all throughout the province.

The idea was to try to encourage clubs to pool their resources. It worked very well, until the first National Coach was appointed in 1982.

Norman Brook came in from Scotland, and he took the whole coaching structure out. He put his own system in.

"We tried to help him, feeling it would not work in Northern Ireland," said Sean.

"We had the system going whereby there was coaching, just not in Belfast and Antrim, at the two tartan tracks there, but also coaching at other centres such as Coalisland. All through the worst of the "Troubles" in Northern Ireland we had a flourishing and successful system of coaching centres in operation, yet all this was dismantled!

It made me very sad that we once had a team of coaches at Ballymena and Antrim AC we would take to different places to encourage the local coaches. A stop was put to that.

"We were trying to develop the coaches as well as the athletes. That system worked superbly well.

I am still meeting coaches, to this day, who tell me they remember when we went to such and such a venue, and how important it all was. Sadly, it was decided coaching was not worth doing, and that is why athletics wandered.

There are four structures in athletics - Administrators, Technical Officials, Coaches and Athletes. You would not have the sport but for the athletes. You would not have quality athletes but for the coaches. So, it has to be coach-athlete centred. Technical Officials and Administrators are in support of that."

137

From 1962 to 1982, Sean Kyle was the official Northern Ireland national coach to the Women's Association before Norman Brook was appointed. In 1963 there was no coaching at all in the Republic of Ireland before Jack Sweeney, who was a lecturer at UCD, set up The Summer School, which was held at UCD. Sean had run his in the winter of 1962 at Gormanstown.

"Those were the first moves to make coaching official in the Republic, now they have their own coaching systems, at all levels - One, Two, Three and Four," said Sean.

"People have to come to realise it all came from 1963. But, we lost what we set up, yet retained the UK coaching system, which administers examinations.

Still, the actual practical side of coaching, of the development of the coaches, is gone here - and that is a tragedy. That is why the standards are as awful as they are."

"There is not a high jump coach other than myself in Northern Ireland," added Maeve.

Despite the obvious irritations, the unstinted Kyle dedication continues to reap reward in the Ballymena and Antrim AC regimes.

"We are proud we still have elite athletes surfacing at the Club, and this is very satisfying," Maeve insists.

"Making great strides is sprinter Anna Boyle, in the 100m and 200m. She has very good potential, as has Lesley Leung. He is majoring in the long jump, the triple jump, and also the sprint. He is a brilliant prospect. There is also Sean McMahon, who competes in the long and triple jumps. He is a good all rounder. We have some brilliant young high jumpers; Caolin Flanagan from Coalisland, Gary Coulter and Clare Wilkinson.

It is hard to tell with young kids, how far they can go in their respective disciplines. You have to be patient. Girls between the ages of 14 and 17 can change shape five times in that period. Boys don't change shape as much, but they grow so fast.

We have the high-jumping lad Coulter, who reached six feet three inches tall when 14 years of age, and took a shoe size of 11.5. Gary proved to be very well co-ordinated to begin with, which is unusual for a child of 14. All he wants to do is athletics. At this school he is not allowed to do high jumps, no weights, no circuits, because it could affect his rugby!

He wants to do athletics, which he does in his spare time, just not at school."

Sean - Antrim Borough Council, Coach of the Year, 1990s

Maeve insists coaching is made up of two parts - the artistic side and the scientific side, but despairs of the modern trend of moving away from old tried and trusted ideals on the subject.

139

She argues: "Unfortunately, in the last number of years it seems you cannot be a coach unless you are qualified in all the scientific side of things. They have forgotten, or overlooked, the coach as the artiste who understands people - who draws out the best from athletes and develops their potential. You can see it in other sports, when you have guys who have never been on a coaching course in their lives - and yet have been the greatest teachers ever! Conversely, you will see guys with all the qualifications in the world, yet they don't seem able to adequately communicate with the pupil, and cannot make him or her any better.

Fluidity in an athlete's style and ability is one of the main ingredients. This has to be nurtured. I am a scientist by profession, and I would be the first to say we need to understand how science can contribute to sport. However, we don't need to let knowledge of sport science determine our sport. That, unfortunately, is what is happening, to a large degree. I think that is very sad. There are people like Steve Cram's coach, Jimmy Henley, who was unqualified yet produced Olympic medallist after Olympic medallist.

He must have been doing something right. The problem is the coaches nowadays believe in their own publicity, that they must be the best. Level Four Coach is the highest you can achieve, yet at the same time I feel the sport is hung up on qualifications. Some coaches have full qualifications, yet really cannot coach because they didn't have the basic natural grounding to gain proper experience.

We are hooked on qualifications in general, and not only in sport. If an athlete is not enjoying his or her sport, and not enjoying trying to be better than he or she is, you cannot impose a system on the athlete. The athlete has to want to be coached, want to improve, want to be better. One of our present club youngsters is a good example. Sean McMahon comes here to our house, and does the weights on his own in the gym. He is a student at the Ballymena Technical College, and he wants to be the best.

Frank Dick, the guru of coaches in England who has supervised many sporting people outside of athletics such as ice skater Katerina Witt and tennis legend Boris Becker, put it in a nutshell. He sums up what I think is the value of coaching when he stated; 'sport will not be successful unless it is athlete-centred and athletes have to be coach-led'. He is quite right. I was taught golf at 14 years of age by the club professional at the Kilkenny Club. The club professional is the coach in golf, and generally still is. That is the way it should be in athletics.

I have been monitoring three sprint coaches at the Club, and every time I go out I have at least two of them with me. I am also entering one high jump coach, and Sean has three middle-distances coaches. All have good qualifications. They are developing their personal confidence, to be able to take sessions and tell people what to do."

140

Kids Stuff

Over the decades, many thousands of athletes have passed through the portals of the Ballymena and Antrim AC, and invariably the process resulted in avid attention to detail by Sean and Maeve in relation to the coaching of kids. The assembly line generally started at schools' level. This has always been a prime issue. Sean was involved for many years at various levels of coaching within school systems, ranging from cross-country events to regular Track and Field competition.

From the early 70's, he was repeatedly involved as a referee or a senior official at all Schools' competition, ranging from various District events to the Ulster Schools' finals, and also in All-Ireland championships. When the British Schools' International came to the Malone track, in 1966, he was the referee - a post he regularly filled when the International came to Ireland.

Maeve was also heavily involved, in charge of the High Jump tests at all the different levels. Both Sean and Maeve have been awarded Tailteann medals from the All-Ireland Schools' Association in recognition of their respective contributions to schools' competition. Generally, there was double award for the intrepid duo, as the Ballymena and Antrim club fostered many schools' champions at Irish level.

One of Maeve's proudest moments, as a coach, was the winning of the coveted Schools' Overall Trophy when she was a teacher at Cambridge House School in Ballymena. Those were times when the facilities for training featured a tarmac playground and a sand pit at one end. From such humble beginnings, and against all odds, emerged British High jump champion and Commonwealth Games silver medallist Sharon McPeake.

From those pioneering days of athletics in the Ballymena area, the emphasis increased in relation to orderly coaching of youngsters. The Club accepted a generous offer from Ballymena Borough Council, sharing with the Council the establishment of a new post of Development Officer. The target is to deliver fundamental training to pupils at Primary level. This is the hoped-for attempt to provide something of a link that is missing in most Primary schools.

The Club has a well-attended weekly group of tiny tots, ranging from kids as young as three years of age to ten year olds who participate in a Fundamental Programme. It is accepted many will drop out, yet a hard core will remain - and progress to higher levels of competition. The Kyles also maintain, in their experience, many so-termed "drop-outs" at this age level later return. They are well schooled in the concept of athletics, and can become good competitors, and indeed develop in other sports.

141

Norman Brook N.I. Nat. Coach, Meave and George Glasgow, Sports Council

"Not many members of the Ballymena and Antrim Club are involved in coaching at schools' level. It has been mainly Maeve and I," said Sean.

"It used to be that Ballymena town had a half day on a Saturday for the offices, as distinct from the shops. Suddenly it was switched. Offices were closed on a Saturday, and open all day on a Wednesday, which was the half day for the shops - who then opened all day Saturday.

It was a bit confusing for a spell. Anyhow, it meant I had more time on hand - and therefore I became more and more involved in school's athletics."

Sean became referee, and has been the Schools International referee since 1966. Maeve was brought into the schools' arena to officiate' usually at the high jump.

While teaching at Cambridge House there were separate girls' and schoolboys' athletic associations. Heather Neeson, from Victoria College, Jim Shaw, from Coleraine Inst, and Maeve managed to put together a structure for a Federation for Schools Athletics in Ulster.

Fresh Frontiers

Maeve was forever attempting to conquer fresh frontiers, and achieved an almost forgotten milestone near the Tundra when the Ballymena and Antrim club took off on summer tour to compete in the unofficial first Bislet Games in 1963. The trip took the small group to Oslo, Bergen and Trondheim - well inside the Arctic Circle. The athletes, and coach Sean Kyle, stayed at Maisingstet, and still receive Christmas cards every year from the family they stayed with up in the mountains. The journey to Norway included competition in an event that was to become world famous.

The Bislet Stadium at Oslo was used for speed skating at the Winter Olympics. Arne Haukuik, who died aged 76 in 2002, founded the official Bislet Games in 1965, and the tournament is now a part of the IAAF Golden League. Ballymena athletes were unwitting pioneers in this venture. Lorna McGarvey and Maeve Kyle ran in the sprints. Maeve set a Scandinavian record time in the 400 metres, to beat the previous all-comers best of Shirley Hampton.

The meeting mainly involved top Norwegian and English athletes, including Adrian Metcalfe. There was a special award for the top athlete of the event, and the gong for "Athlete of the Meet" went to Maeve!

This was one of the early highlights of the restless breed from Ballymena, always willing to test skills on foreign fields. Maeve, especially, enjoyed personal

143

Canada tour, 1988

globetrotting at the highest competitive level, and up to present time the great lady is almost constantly on the move to assist Ballymena and Antrim AC's young prospects compete in all corners of the universe. Aware of the need to encourage and reward the club's young prospects, and also the experienced athletes, for honest hard endeavour and further cement the family bonding atmosphere, Maeve and Sean first decided in 1961 to take the club show on the road. It proved a marvellous incentive as the Ballymena ambassadors of sport embarked on world travel. The beginnings, however, were of the humble variety.

The Club tours started in Scotland in 1961, at Maryhill. It was the first trip for the Club, and around 50 athletes and officials went to a meeting against what is now Glasgow AC.

After Norway, it was back to Scotland in 1967 - a trip that was to prove a very interesting and productive one. The Club cemented great contacts there, as it turned out later on - as Northern Ireland moved deeper into unrest, the one and only team to come regularly to Northern Ireland throughout the worst of the Troubles was the Scottish Women's Athletics team.

"The Scottish female athletes competed at Ormeau Park every year, seniors and juniors," said Sean. "I suggested a match with these people while in

144

Scotland. It was brilliant. It was very, very important at that time, because it kept sport alive in Northern Ireland. Generally, sport was great right through the Troubles, although some sports struggled and found it difficult because they couldn't get people willing to come in from outside the country."

In 1973, the Club went Dutch, with a party of 50 travelling to Arnhem. In 1975, the Club travelled to Dusseldorf arriving at 8 o'clock at night, dead tired.

Maeve takes up the story: "The Germans asked us if were a mixed team, I said yes - meaning boys and girls. We were to stay in private houses. The kids were very tired and fed up with the delay. I asked if there was a problem, and the reply was - yes. The German hosts wanted to know which members of the team were Catholic and which were Protestant! They did not want to put them together in case they would fight if placed in the one house. Sadly, that was the image we portrayed on television abroad in those days."

In 1984, it was back to Holland and Germany and in 1988 the Club again travelled to Canada having previously been there in 1979. In 1991, 1992 and 1993 it was closer to home with the Club's athletes competing in the Jersey Games at St Hellier.

However Ballymena and Antrim AC truly stamped their international passport through their two Canadian expeditions, and the Kyles are justifiably proud of the ambitious trans-Atlantic tours.

Irish Team, Japan, 1997

Lizzie McWilliams - Junior Commonwealth Games, Bendigo, 2004

Sean watching Eddie King - World Juniors 1986

Sean meeting HRH Prince Edward, 1981

Anna Boyle

Sharon McPeake,
Auckland 1990

Club on tour, Cyprus 1997

Sean and Maeve at home, 1988

Receiving the Irish Schools Tailteann Award, 1994

5th July 2006 at the Waterfront Hall in Belfast, Maeve Kyle, Chair of Coaching Northern Ireland, received the degree of Doctor of the University in recognition of her distinction as a sportswomen and her work in the development of coaching. Maeve received her award from the Chancellor of the University of Ulster, Sir Richard Nichols.

Sean and Maeve after receiving her Honourary Doctorate

The Kyle family with Maeve after receiving her Doctorate at University of Ulster 2006.

Roberta Murray, Antrim Forum Manager, & guests at the 2012 Roadshow at the Antrim Forum

Antrim Forum, home of Ballymena & Antrim Athletic Club since 1979

Steve Cram and Ana Boyle with children at the 2012 Roadshow

Gary Coulter, Richard Browning, Maeve, Anna Boyle and Claire Wilkinson, Antrim Forum, 2006

Maeve Kyle with Steve Cram, Antrim Forum, 2006

Having a laugh, Sydney Olympics 2000

Recent times, Shauna, Maeve and Sean at Sean's 80th birthday celebrations, December 2006

Sean with Wilson Kipketer (World 800m Record Holder) and Ricky Simms (Wilson Kipketer's Manager)

UTV's Adrian Logan with Maeve and Sean

Maeve with Lord Coe, Coaching NI, Coach of the Year Awards, 2006

Maeve with Jim Gourley, Lord Coe and Coaching NI Chief Executive, Stephen Maguire

Maeve and Sean at home at Tir-na-nOg

Sonia O'Sullivan with Maeve

Endless Accolades

The summer of 2006 brought added honours to the endless array of deserved accolades for the Kyles, with Maeve receiving a special Ulster University award in July. She is now Dr Maeve Kyle, following an honorary doctorate at Jordanstown, in recognition of her distinction as a sportswoman and her work in the development of coaching.

Maeve was also appointed to the Northern Ireland Task Force for the 2012 London Olympics.

"It looks as if it could be very interesting," she said. *"I have been asked to join the Committee that will look after the volunteers. A huge number of people from Northern Ireland have applied to be volunteers. It is basically to try and see what strategy we would have, to get a united front on how Northern Ireland can be involved in the 2012 Olympics - and what the spin-off is for Northern Ireland.*

The Task Force, headed here by Mike Corry who is in the Department of Culture, Arts and Leisure [DCAL], is also for finding kids who have the potential to be champions. I am not saying Olympic champions, but champions who would make Olympic teams.

That is not necessarily the kids who are winning at this stage. It is the kids who are in the system, 16 year olds who are showing real commitment to being the best. The coaching legacy will probably be the most important of all from the 2012 Olympics. It is about what will stay after. There is a lot of work

Sebastian Coe, Los Angeles Olympics 1984

involved in the new sports strategy, and that will also involve a new coaching strategy, for the UK and for Ireland."

Elevation to high office came after years of dedication to athletics. Maeve was a first female member of the Jury of Appeal at the 1982 Games in Brisbane.

During the early 1980's Maeve was team manager of a Great Britain and Northern Ireland team competing against Italy in Sardinia, but it was far from plain sailing . . . instead it was drama all the way, with airport officials virtually shredding poles for the tournament at Cagliari.
"We took a big plane to Rome, and then switched to a smaller aeroplane for the remainder of the journey to Cagliari," said Maeve.

"When we went to collect the poles, stowed in a special baggage section, the airport handlers presented us with two very large parcels of neatly sawed-in-half poles. The poles were 14 feet long and did not fit into the small hold...so some official decided there was but one solution . . . to cut the 24 poles by half the length. This proved no problem in loading, only of no use for competition.

We reached a compromise with the Italian officials after we declared there would be no pole vaulting match unless we could borrow the Italian team's poles. They agreed to share and our boys won that event.

We all had a good laugh, and the insurance eventually paid for new poles. From the late 1970s on, I was a Senior Manager for British teams. I was also in line for GB Olympic team manager in 1988. Somehow politics got in the way - ironically from the Northern Ireland Athletic Association! Representatives from NIAA voted against me, which was a bit sad as everyone else decided I was the one.

On a happier note, part of the selection process was to manage senior athletes at every level of competition, and I was asked to take a small team to a big meeting in Florence in 1983. The team included Sebastian Coe and very young Fatima Whitbread. It proved a very successful expedition."

Many times Maeve has served as Team Leader for Great Britain and for Ireland, and was coach for the sprint and relay teams at the Sydney Olympics of 2000.

Both Sean and Maeve continue to serve as coaches and Technical Officials to British and Irish teams at Europa Cup meetings.

Fatima Whitbread excelled under the Maeve's mangement

161

Looking Back.....Moving Forward

You could have heard a pin drop as both Sean and Maeve informed their members that they were about to step back. It was time to begin to let go. A defining moment in the Club's history arrived. Everybody knew it had to come some day, but maybe tomorrow, because tomorrow never comes - and life without the guiding hands of Maeve and Sean seemed unthinkable. A sharp intake of breath greeted the decision - the security blanket prized away from the extended Kyle family..

Phillip Snoddy, a former athletic protégé and now one of the senior Grade 3 coaches destined to carry the Club forward, sat at the Annual General Meeting. This was one of those days he and the other Club members would not forget.

A watershed, as Phillip explained: "It was a sad moment, at the AGM, when Maeve announced that both she and Sean were having to take a step back from running the club. It was a realisation that things weren't right; after all they are Ballymena and Antrim Athletic Club," he said.

"You realise they were the original life-coaches, even before this phrase came into vogue. Not only looking after the athlete, but also coaching the person, whether promoting the importance of exams, or advising on life changing decisions, as well as being a shoulder to cry on, they nudged athletes into life

162

Johnny Kilpatrick
Coached by Sean 1962-1971
Irish Junior champion and schools
international. Full Irish International
from 1964.
World Student Games GB Budapest
1965. Ran in 4X100m relay.
Commonwealth Games 1966 and
1970. N. Ireland reached final of
4X100 m relay.
British International Indoors 1970 and
anchored GB to victory in 4X100m
relay against East Germany
Northern Ireland Champion and 4
times record holder at 100 yds as well
as 220 yds and long jump titles. Twice
Irish Champion and record holder at
100 yds.

pathways. The Kyles promoted an environment of acceptance - when you stepped into the arena you were there for sport - yet you picked up so much more.

Last summer, I brought my son down to the track - and while coming away Sean stopped for a chat. His chats are legendary, once you get him started. Unfortunately for my son, when asked by Sean if he enjoyed himself, replied that he liked the throwing events, in particular the javelin.

Sean then proceeded to give a personal 10-minute lecture on the art of the javelin to my son - twisting him this way and that, and pointing out the finer techniques. Any elite javelin thrower would have reveled in this, but as he pointed out, even if my son remembers just a few points they're in his head for life. That's very true, once you've met this extraordinary couple, that meeting will stick in your memory."

Johnny Kilpatrick, a sporting club icon of the 1960's and 1970's, looked back at the changing face of sport and his time with the Kyles. Sean and Maeve's decision to 'step back' was the topic of discussion in many households, with Johnny mulling over many glorious memories of a golden yesteryear.

'Athletics in my time was not as professional as now, and I was able to mix athletics with rugby, playing for Ballymena and Ulster. We had no funding and on many occasions relied on the time, generosity and transport of Sean and Maeve

Lorna McGarvey and Maeve, 1965

to get to venues. Without their enthusiasm Ballymena Athletic Club might not have survived," he said.

"Sean was my coach, turning out in all weathers to conduct sessions. You did sport for the love of it in those days. I remember well, training on a rough cinder path behind his house in Leighinmohr Avenue, and there were the weekly circuit training evenings during the winter in the gym at the Demesne.

I was a student in Belfast, travelled to Ballymena every week, and took a lift in Pauline Hoolbrook's mini, along with Kate Hoey - now a Labour MP and former-Sports Minister who was a student at Jordanstown.

I remember the Saturday training on the Queen's track at Malone, and still recall the pain of repeated hill runs. At these sessions, Sean coached not only athletes from Ballymena but also almost all of the leading track athletes in the North. I remember the trips also to Portstewart, to train in the sand hills, and also going to train at Gormanstown.

Sean was a great motivator, and he knew exactly when to drive hard and when a bit of sympathy would go better. He even managed to get a reasonable degree of fitness in me. No easy task, as I was never the most enthusiastic trainer, but I thrived on competition. I have never known Sean to lose his temper with an athlete.

By post, Sean coached and gave readily of his advice to athletes around the world. Indeed I know of no couple that has a better network of friends in the athletics world.

I believe their friends threw a great dinner for them a few years ago in Greece, to celebrate Sean's birthday. Just shows the respect they have for him.

However, like a prophet, Sean is not always respected in his own land!

Then there was the Kyles' house. A more athletic house you could not believe - and it still is. Maeve was a fellow athlete at that time, and had not yet branched out as a coach in her own right.

Never folk to flow with the stream, they had their own strong views how athletics should be run, and they were never afraid to express them. Indeed, they had views on most sports.

After some 35 years away from Northern Ireland, I find their house is just the same today; athletics centred - and somewhere you can drop into as if you never had been away, and pick up the conversation where you left off... even if it was five years ago."

Lorna Kerr (nee McGarvey) and Johnny Kilkpatrick both made the trip to Jamacia for the 1966 Commonwealth Games, but special memories are not just about competing. Lorna has not forgotten her first meeting with Maeve, her hockey links, an abiding friendship and a trip to Norway among other little snap shots of past adventures.

"I first met Maeve during a young athletes' course at Stranmillis Training College, Belfast, in 1961. I was 17, and Maeve was an instructor on the course. and even then an Irish sporting legend. Maeve asked if I would be interested in joining Ballymena Athletics Club. I was so thrilled. I couldn't believe it. I had been desperate to join an athletics club, but a girl at school, who was a member, told me you had to be invited to join - and that seemed quite out of my reach.

That summer, after training evenings under Sean's watchful eye on the old cinder track at the Showgrounds, it would be back to The Kyles for bacon and egg. Sean would then drive me from Ballymena to meet my father coming from Portstewart.

They were unbelievably generous with their time and commitment.

We became close friends. Their home became my second home, and everything I achieved in athletics was due to their friendship and Sean's coaching skill. We had an unforgettable three-week holiday in Norway, in 1963. We ran in every

Club trip to Canada, 1979

athletics meeting taking place in Norway, at that time. I travelled the length of that beautiful country, and a new world opened up to me.

Sean coached me as a young schoolgirl, and under his guidance I became an Irish international. I also represented Great Britain in the World Student Games of 1965, and Northern Ireland in the Commonwealth Games at Jamaica in 1966. None of this would have happened without the friendship and encouragement of Maeve and Sean.

Back then, I was also challenging Maeve for the position of left wing in the Ulster and Irish hockey teams. We had great fun playing alongside each other every week for Instonians, and for a short period we even took it in turns to play left wing in the Irish team. The rivalry between us never became a problem in our friendship, and Maeve's constant support was always invaluable.

Although I left Northern Ireland in 1966, to live abroad in Hong Kong where I had a teaching post, I have never forgotten their dedication and the enormous generosity and friendship shown to me as a young athlete. I owe them both so much and have such wonderful memories of the times we shared. I thank them most sincerely for everything they did for me. What an incredible partnership and

166

what an inspiration they have been to so many young people in their lifetime. Their place in Irish sport must surely be unique."

Raymond Knox created another club milestone when he established his international pedigree as a British decathlete competing at the 1974 Commonwealth Games. His grooming for success was masterminded by Sean, and he reckons his former coach should not be overlooked for a special award.

"His dedication to sport is immense, and deserves the highest recognition. This is not to diminish the contribution of Maeve. Whereas she has often been in the limelight as a competitor, Sean has been working tirelessly in the background, coaching and organising at club and international level. Athletics will be the poorer when he finally retires.

Without Sean's coaching and encouragement I would never have been the athlete I was. I joined Ballymena Athletic Club when I was at Queen's University, and I will always remember his dedication in coming to Belfast several days a week to coach a variety of athletic disciplines.

Also, their home was always, and still is, open to any athlete who wanted to avail of their hospitality.

To compete in a sport, you have to enjoy the sport - and it is largely due to my involvement in Ballymena and Antrim Athletic Club and the help and support of Sean and Maeve that I competed for the period that I did."

Mark Kirk - Middle distance ace, has a few recollections of travel to fascinating destinations.

"I joined Ballymena Athletic Club back in the 1970's, when I was 10 years old, and trained at Ballymena Academy twice a week. Maeve looked after us, and we all had great fun. It was a great introduction to athletics, and many of us stayed in athletics and competed at senior level. Some of us still compete today.

When I think back on my athletics career, I really appreciate the time and effort that Maeve and Sean put in to help me pursue my athletic dreams. They were so dedicated to the club.

They used to give me lifts to training, two or three times a week, and maybe to a race at the weekend. As well as that, we travelled the length and breadth of Ireland.

Some of these journeys were memorable, not only for Maeve's exciting driving but also because of whom we had to share the car with.

Maeve and Sean would normally each bring their cars to training. It was always preferable to travel with Sean. In Maeve's car you had to share with a huge dog. The trick was to try and get the front seat as the dog tended to stand between the two front seats with its rear end facing the back. If you were unfortunate enough to get the middle seat in the back the view and the smell was most unpleasant.

My abiding memory of Sean would be his voice. He had the loudest voice in athletics. If he saw you beginning to slip back in a race your ears would ring with the sound of his voice shouting encouragement.

It was always a useful tool for keeping you focused during training sessions. He has a great knack of getting the best out of you, both in both racing and training - and had a penchant to pick you up with a few kind words when things were not going so well.

One thing I always dreaded though was when he presented you with your latest training schedule. He showed the master plan for the coming months. All those training sessions were laid out in front of you, for you to tackle in the future.

No matter how hard it seemed we always managed to do it under his watchful eye, of course.

Melanie Browning (nee Fee) returned to the fold to coach at the club. "I first knew Maeve and Sean during the mid 1970's, when I was a young sprinter with the Club. My association with the Club was relatively brief, six years, but I thoroughly enjoyed my time there. Maeve and Sean were constant figures at the Club. They looked after all their athletes just like 'surrogate parents'. I remember in 1979, the Club organised a trip to Toronto, Canada. I thought my parents were unable to afford my fare, so I never put my name forward to go. Maeve, being Maeve, noticed this, and without a hesitation called my mother and offered to pay my fare.

Fortunately my 16th birthday brought with it the fruition of an insurance policy - and I did go on the trip. I enjoyed the experience of a lifetime. To watch the World Championships, and in particular the great Ed Moses, is something I will always treasure. My thanks to Maeve and Sean for the opportunity, and the memories. Through my athletics, competing throughout the UK as part of various Northern Ireland teams, I enjoyed a wonderful education through traveling, meeting other athletes and making new friends. Reflecting on that time now, I wouldn't have had all of those experiences without Maeve and Sean behind me, encouraging me.

To them, I say thanks for a wonderful teenage life.

In recent years, my eldest son developed an interest in athletics. I took him down to Ballymena and Antrim Athletic Club. I couldn't believe Maeve and Sean were still there - and still continuing to encourage and inspire young athletes.

With the help of Maeve, I am now actively involved as a coach, with my husband too - and only hope that we can give the encouragement and enthusiasm that I was shown at that age. Maeve and Sean are a true inspiration to us all of what can be achieved through continuous commitment and dedication.'

One by one, story after story, a common theme emerged from athletes, colleagues, friends and family...their extended Kyle family.

Pauline Thom (nee Quinn) is part of the extended Kyle family. It was more than sport; it was about embracing and shaping people. Sport was the vechicle. Maeve and Sean the driving force. Pauline met future husband Dougie Thom through the Club. "Maeve and Sean acted like my second set of parents. Not only were they excellent coaches, but also they had a genuine concern for my overall well-being, education, and place in society. This wasn't something unusual, they were like this to every athlete. Maeve would call us all her 'adopted family'.

Sean was the middle distance coach, and during my teenage years at the club he had a very strong squad of athletes. Two weeks before the Northern Ireland trials for the World Cross-country Championships in Warsaw, Poland, in 1987, Sean asked me if I had a passport, as I could possibly make the team. I didn't, as the furthest I'd been in my life was a school trip to London. He quickly arranged for me to get a passport - nothing ever seemed to be much trouble to Sean or Maeve, they were always there to help. Unfortunately I didn't make this team. However, once I had that passport, my confidence soared and Sean made me realise that I could make International teams and travel to many parts of the world.

When I look at my passport, and see all the countries I have visited through athletics, Japan, Hong Kong, Portugal, Canada, Spain, Greece to name but a few, I can only thank Sean and Maeve for providing me with these opportunities.

One trip to Canada gives an insight into how we all respected and listened to every word the Kyles spoke. One evening, Maeve gave us a lecture on how our nightly visits to McDonald's would prove detrimental to our performance. We needed to eat more 'wholesome' foods. My friend Kerry and I decided Maeve was right, and we found a Japanese restaurant not far from our hotel in Ottawa. After being seated and handed a menu in our very posh restaurant, Kerry looked at me and said "Pauline, have you seen the prices!"

Pauline Quinn aged 15, with Sean

Needless to say we left the restaurant hungrier than ever, after a starter each. That was all we could afford. Arriving back at the hotel and reciting this tale, Maeve couldn't stop herself from laughing as she explained she was only suggesting that we went for Pizza or Pasta at Pizza Hut or similar eatery rather than eat burgers every night.

Sean and Maeve's commitment to athletics has never floundered over the years. They even turned their garage into a gym so athletes could do weight training - I think Maeve would have had other ideas for her garage!

The Kyles' garage became a twice-weekly source of entertainment and gossip. Sean was always at hand to instruct and advise us.

Once he suffered a very bad cold, the snow was on the ground and the ice was forming on the inside of the garage windows. Maeve was scolding Sean for sitting in the garage as we did our weights. However, Sean has 'selective hearing' - and he continued to monitor our weights programme, an example of his dedication.

The highlight of my athletics career was not all the championship medals I won or any of my international selections, but when Sean chose me to attend the athletic awards in the Savoy Hotel, London.

Sean won the UK Coach of the Year title, and was able to bring two athletes to the function, all expenses paid.

This was a great honour, as he had coached many talented international runners. On the night I rubbed shoulders with many Olympians and track stars such as Roger Black, Kriss Akabussi and Sally Gunnell – a proud moment for a 15 year old girl from Ballymena.

Anna Boyle, who began her sporting experiences on the gaelic fields of Dunloy, including a brief spell as an under-16 county camogie player, was introduced to the Kyles by Catherine Magee. The principal of St Patrick's College spotted Anna's athletic potential during earlier years at Our Lady of Lourdes Secondary School, Ballymoney.

Anna quickly mushromed to become one of the pride and joy members of the Club. She is significantly a sprint double and kindred spirit of her ever-devoted coach Maeve. It is as if the past track attacks, that made Maeve so famous, are manifesting themselves through the outstanding prospect from north Antrim.

There is, however. much more to the successes, in the 60m, 100m and 200m, and the close harmony that is the cornerstone of the renowned Ballymena and Antrim AC.

"It has been an amazing and hugely exciting journey for me, ever since my parents took me to the Ballymena and Antrim club.

I first took an interest in running, while in P6 at Our Lady of Lourdes' School, Ballymoney, and won a few races.

I won the 100 metres at both the Ulster Schools and All Ireland Schools' championships. I also competed in the high and long jumps, and also played camogie.

I was keen to improve as much as possible in athletics. Since then, it has been a wonderful experience.

I was 14 when I met them. I knew they would play a huge role in my life, as their presence and motivation inspired me right from the start. Maeve became my coach, and quickly made me realise it was athletics I wanted to succeed in.

In the last nine years I have done much in terms of work relationships and sport. Sean and Maeve have been mentors to me, and have a fantastic relationship with my parents. Guiding me so well in all of life's challenges I feel that fate decides the people that shape your life. Maeve and Sean have done that, not only through sport but my studies. I achieved a 2:2 this year in my Degree. While spending six weeks in Melbourne competing at the Commonwealth Games, they played a

Maeve with Anna Boyle
172

huge role in advising me how to balance all the little things in life, such as work, study and sport. I have travelled to various countries with Maeve and Sean, and will never forget the year we all went to South Africa. It was Maeve's third trip, and Sean's first. It is a precious memory I will hold forever. We had a ball. I gained more education during the 16 days there than in my four years at university ... in terms of sport, life, relationships, experiences.

The Kyles live for each other, and after 52 years of marriage are still so much in love - as can be seen every day. The Club is an extension of their own family. They treat all the members equally. That is the main reason why the Club has been so successful. The friendships made I will treasure forever.

Sean and Maeve looked after me in every way possible. It is the same for every Club member. Not only are we coached in whatever disciplines we are keen to progress in, but also Maeve and Sean take a personal interest in everything we do, our education.

Their influence on my track career, and also on my education and outlook on life, is simply remarkable.

The Kyles are phenomenal. I don't think it is possible to adequately put in words their contribution to athletics. Maeve and Sean have done so much for me, and it goes beyond coaching or racing. They are unbelievable and offer the same advice and help to all members in the Club.

There is a tremendous family spirit in the Club. The Kyles are so whole-hearted about athletics it instantly rubs off on a new member at the club, and it takes off from there. Their enthusiasm is infectious. The Ballymena and Antrim Club is the Kyles' extended family. You can go to their house in Ballymena at any time to seek help and advice. They never turn you away, whether you are one of the club's top performers or a struggling athlete.

It is 'open house' at all times to club members. What should not be overlooked is the fact they help in every way possible - to improve your outlook on life, to respect others. They take an abiding interest in every club member, both on and off the track, educate you on life away from athletics, on how to be a good person, what is the right thing to do.

I have travelled all over the world with the Kyles to compete in team meetings and championships, and they always look out for me, seeking out what is in my best interests".

John Stewart, the Ballymena and Antrim AC President since 1996, is a retired headmaster of St Louis Grammar School, Ballymena, and holds a respected insight to the pride, thinking, workings, energy and the unselfish devotion Sean and Maeve retain for the Club.

"The dynamism given to the Club by Sean and Maeve is phenomenal. The two of them are remarkable. Their enthusiasm and drive never diminishes. They have created an infrastructure of support, people who help out in a voluntary capacity - many of whom are good qualified coaches. I am sure those people will take over in the future.

The circuit-training programme, and the running sessions in Portglenone Forest, brings in young people from numerous places. The parents are very supportive, and this is a crucial part of the Club's solid structure.

Youngsters are also developing social skills, high levels of self-confidence, poise, and of course improving their athletic potential. I witnessed many excellent youngsters progress through the system to become very good athletes. I have seen how academic performances have been enhanced because of the commitment to the training schedule. Taking on board the circuit training on a Tuesday evening is as tough as anything. Sean Kyle developed a unique circuit-training programme, and up to eighty people do this throughout the winter months.

I have been associated with the Club since 1975, when I started going to the circuit training, which was then staged at Ballymena Academy, and on a Tuesday evening. It has been at St Louis Grammar for the last eight years. It is an interesting point that when Sean decided to stop going to Ballymena Academy, for the Tuesday evening winter circuit-training programme, he came to me in 1998 and asked if they could use the facilities at St Louis.

"I brought Sean to St Louis Grammar on the 15th August 1998, to show him what was available. The reason I remember the date is it was the day of the dreadfully appalling bomb at Omagh. If there was any reason for the Club to be in a school, and a Catholic school too, that was the time - and it also sent out the message the school facility was open to everybody, and the Club is open to everybody, too. Frank Cassidy, my successor at St Louis keeps it going.

Noleen McConnell (nee McGarvey) is another famous name with an illustrious sporting past. She is Honorary President of NEBSSA (North Eastern Board School Sport Association), and mirrored the feelings of so many former athletes whose lives were shaped by their association with the Ballymena & Antrim Club.

Noleen and was passionate in her praise of the remarkable double act that relentlessly drives the Club forward.

174

N.I. Commonwealth games 400m Relay Finalists
Lynsey Teskey, Maeve, Noleen McGarvey, Adelene Smith

'Where would athletics be in Northern Ireland without the influence of the Kyles? How many of us would have reached our personal bests or competed at such a high level without their support and guidance over so many years. I know I have to thank them for all they did for me - the encouragement they offered in my International career, and included was the unstinting help to achieve my main goal of representing Northern Ireland at the Commonwealth Games.

The life of an athlete is a very lonely one. Every achievement is so personal, every failure hits home hard, and the Kyles were always there to celebrate everyone's successes, and also encourage them to try again, when they were disappointed with their performance.

This book will be full of personal thanks, but I would mainly like to praise them for all the work that they have done in starting so many young people on the road to success. This support has been given unselfishly down through the decades. The North Eastern Board School Sport Association has always been very grateful to Maeve and Sean for attending so many NEBSSA Athletic finals and also NEBSSA cross-country Championships. They brought their vast expertise to these events, and have always willingly officiated at the competitions. It was during these Championships, Sean and Maeve were able to spot future athletes and invite them to attend the training sessions at Ballymena & Antrim Athletics Club. While some fell by the wayside, many went on to compete for the Club, and

175

many competed for their country. This is true Talent Identification, from school to the club. Anna Boyle is one of many young athletes who competed in the NEBBSA competitions that owe so much to both Maeve and Sean. They spotted her talent, and made sure she was given every opportunity that was available.

I believe that the greatest achievement of the Kyle's has been their ability to identify children at an early age, giving them all the encouragement they needed - and setting them on the road to reach their personal best at whatever level they managed to achieve.

Sharon Hutchings (nee McPeake)

Commonwealth Silver Medalist

I still call them Mr and Mrs Kyle, and not by their first names. At the age of 44 it illustrates how much respect I still have for them. My first memory of Mrs Kyle goes back to when I was about twelve years age, when she became my relief geography teacher at Cambridge House School.

In those days, I did a bit of long jump and hurdling, as well as high jumping. Mrs Kyle also started taking students for games lessons, and thought I could become a good athlete with a bit of coaching. Little did she know what she was letting herself in for. When it was time for after-school coaching, I would send one of my friends to the front door to see if she was waiting for me - and then I would leg it out the back door, and onto the bus.

I managed to escape a few times, but she cottoned on to what was happening - and caught me out. Thank God she did, as I would never have become the athlete I was without her perseverance. She then took me to the Club, where I then met Mr Kyle. When I started competing for the Club, and travelling around the country, Mrs Kyle would give me geography lessons in the car. She emphasised the different things I was expected to learn, some of which I remember today - like meandering rivers. She made it all so exciting.

I went on my first big trip at 18 years of age, to Edmonton, Canada, with Mr Kyle. What a ball we had. Do you remember Mr Kyle, when that man in a restaurant wanted to marry me? You were up in arms, saying you were my guardian for the trip and to stay away from me.

My lasting memory, apart from the deepest snow I have ever seen, was the fact that for the two weeks we were there you took to me to a different nationality restaurant every night. What an experience that was. It was the first of many trips I was to take with them over the years, whether it was Club trips to places like Germany - or Games like the Commonwealths. which were usually much further away. Wherever it was, the Kyles always made me feel safe.

Sharon Hutchings, Auckland, 1990

They also made it fun in between training and competing. Mrs Kyle made me believe I could be a good high jumper, and thanks to her I think I was.

I even met my husband Tim through her determination to make me a good athlete. I was introduced to Tim during a warm-weather training camp in Portugal, and she did me the great honour of making my wedding cake a few years later. We have had a few tears and tantrums through the years, mostly mine, but my life has been so much richer from hanging out with such a fantastic, devoted, loving and remarkable couple - the Kyles.

I hope they have very many more happy years, and that those lovely smiles I remember so well never leave their faces. Thank you for everything.

Love Sharon

Epilogue

Maeve may claim to have eased back on her schedule after the heart ailment of 2004, but you would hardly notice the difference. Old habits are difficult to shake off. You can see it in the structured life of the Kyles, whose prime focus is to maintain the success of the Ballymena and Antrim Athletic Club - a monument to their unstinted dedication. There is more to the twin driving force than merely track fact, although their influence spans many facets of Irish athletics and hockey.

This is a good opportunity to try and place the Kyles amid the great progress of sport on this island after World War Two. Their contribution, always a subjective exercise, must be colossal. It is a family thing, with Maeve the focal influence right from her beginnings as Maeve Shankey. Achievements in sport came naturally. Maeve knew no better. How could she? Her parents were sports-loving people who lived through an especially serene time that will, I fear, never be recaptured.

Maeve is justifiably proud of being born into an age of chivalry, and a respecter of Corinthian values. Midway through the 20th century was an era of real money, when every single shilling and penny was made to work to the fullest capacity. It is understandably difficult for the young people of present times to accept that reputations and rewards had to be earned the hard and honest way. There was no queue of Sports Agents armed with bulging financial offers, no Lottery Funding, no sponsorship, no drugs, no state of the art training facilities. It was a

178

Belgrade 1962 European Championships - Tito & Madam Broz

time of good grace, good manners, and credit respectfully accorded to the winner of whatever sporting discipline was at stake.

The life and times of the Kyles is an endless one, and it was a joy to recall the poignant phases. For me this timeless tale began in December 2004. Right away, I knew I was approaching a special place, yet it was not until much later I released how delightfully appropriate was the legend on the entrance gate.

The quirky decision to name the house "Tir-na-nOg" was inspirational, just like everything else the Kyles ventured into during a half-century as an inseparable partnership. Finding the residence for a first time proved difficult, despite detailed instructions over the telephone by that distinctly firm and slightly husky "brogue" that is the inimitable Maeve. Before reaching any opinions, I was not sure what to expect from my first official fact-finding visit to the Kyle house, situated off the Old Galgorm Road, Ballymena.

Their youthful attitude to all things in life, and not just a single focus on athletics, remains just as collectively vibrant now as it was back in the Fifties - when Sean and Maeve first met. They maintain, in their own inimitable fashion, a special and inspired land of the young. There is the continued tireless working for the athletes of tomorrow, yet never losing the nostalgic link with a glorious past.

I was of two minds where this journey would lead, wondering how much substance of an extra special nature there was in the Kyle family devotion to athletics - and their pride and joy, Ballymena and Antrim AC. Many years back, I met Sean and Maeve on a few fleeting occasions, when I had a brief and ill-informed sortie into writing on local athletics.

Maeve Kyle was the queen of the track in those days. My interest in times clocked during competition by Maeve, and all the other high performance detail of achievement and records by other members of the Ballymena and Antrim AC over fifty years, was lukewarm. It seemed to me a potential bore to pen the history of the remarkable Club by sticking merely to athletic prowess.

I was soon to find out Maeve and Sean, the inveterate statistician, agreed. Their life was one of colour, drama, controversy, excitement, sadness, and tales of the unexpected. I drove past Cambridge House a little way. Once over a rise onto a slight gradient I took a sudden left into an unsigned bumpy and rutted lane, dividing select and slumbering houses guarded by impressively old and varied trees.

Launch of NI Sports Council Maeve Ivan Cooper Mary Peters at Stormont, 1970

Once I saw the legend on the gate I knew I was on the right path, and one that would lead to a fascinating adventure. Maeve's mother came up with the name Tir-na-nOg, for a house built in 1966, after leaving the first family home at Leighinmohr Avenue. The devoted partnership of Sean and Maeve Kyle had to develop from rock-solid corner stones, and have especially firm roots. Nostalgia and a respect for tried and trusted values happily proved in healthy state.

They guided me through an extraordinary and very special memory lane, one that started well before the day Ballymena and Antrim AC was born. I felt instantly at ease, in this oasis built in a seemingly ageless old wooded corner of Ballymena's green belt. These were visible signs of old decency. The serene setting of the sprawling house was a little haven secreted well away from the prying eyes of the outside world. It was as if in a time-warp.

The silent pond, and the contrasting aggressive greeting by the unfriendly soundings of a diligent guard dog named Sheeba. Described as "nearly an Alsatian" who had nervously moped into the Kyle Insurance offices many years earlier, in the town centre, the faithful retainer is utterly protective of her twin masters. The grateful family guardian is not alone in receiving the complete welcome from the kind-hearted Kyles, but also stray athletes, who seem to come and go in the conveyer belt use of a specially fitted gymnasium.

Maeve with 1956 Olympic boxers, Johnny Caldwell and Freddie Gilroy - September 2006, City Hall, Belfast

Olympic Opening Ceremony, Tokyo 1964, Maeve's third Olympics

182

The house exuded the feeling of valued history, of well being. There was a veritable Pandora's Box of sporting memorabilia, medals, all sorts and shapes of trophies, photographs - all marking a lifetime of spectacular achievement. The collections of wonderful happenings are related mainly to sporting occasions. There are also links with a glorious past - numerous mementoes, including pictures of a special place reminding Maeve of her upbringing beside Kilkenny College.

There was also the significant feel of orderliness. Sean appeared to have an uncluttered mind, a photographic memory, and an almost endless cache of cuttings and photographs of family, club and individual sporting achievements. Maeve, always with a disarming modesty when it came to highlighting an incident of special significance during her star-studded career in athletics and hockey, had an enthusiastic habit of suddenly straying from one situation of a past exploit to another - and just as suddenly back again.

We would take a leap from one decade to maybe two ahead, and back again. It was wonderful, hugely enjoyable. More often than not, I forgot my reason for being there, to try and etch a serious project on extremely high achievers of the sporting world. Not overly strong on dates and detail, Maeve's generalisations were always filled with warmth and colour. You could close your eyes and picture being right there, involved in the incident. There was always a story behind the statistic.

Maeve and Sean relax at home in Tir-na-nOg

Sean advising young athletics prospects

Form little acorns - Maeve coaches the children

Her childhood memories, from an idyllic upbringing in Kilkenny, had me hypnotised. I knew from the start this was not going to be merely a simple straightforward scribbling chore about sporting success. The lengthy unforgettable yarns unearthed a marvellous mixture of tales of dedication, about how the hugely successful Ballymena and Antrim Club grew from humble beginnings, the unswerving undercurrent of twin dedication to athletics. Sean and Maeve Kyle were, I feel, born with vocations to dedicate their lives to sport.

Also, the love match that brought them together was straight out of fairytale, the quirkily arranged meeting of a man from Ballymena and a girl from Kilkenny. Still, sport was the common denominator. The respect and bonding burns as brightly as ever. There was that matter-of-fact ease throughout all my meetings with the Kyles. Maeve revealed she had to deal with serious illness earlier in 2004. She still looked impressively fresh, fit and youthful for someone who was 76 in October 2004, and just recovering from a heart attack.

Tir-na-nOg, the dogs and Maeve

Sean and Maeve, 1965

Maeve AAA coach

Maeve at home, 1968

The irrepressible female was soon back in full flight, coaching alongside Sean at their beloved Ballymena and Antrim Athletic Club. She had to forego a proposed trip to the summer Olympic Games at Athens, when not up to par because of the on-coming illness, confessing to not feeling great during the previous eighteen months, considering the fatigue part of the ageing process, yet continued to place pressure on herself.

187

Maeve and Sean with granddaughter, Indy, 1998

Timeout. Sean with daughter Shauna and granddaughter Indy

A key to the Kyle success was family time.

Shauna, Sean and Maeve, 1962

Sean and Maeve, August 1953

Maeve did not hide one of her shortcomings, impatience to get things done quickly. It is her way of life, and she probably paid a bit for overstretching. Just when you think Maeve will take a break she comes with wide-eyed information of another fresh and exciting challenge.

Driving away from Tir-na-nOg, I reflected warmly on that first meeting with two exceptional people; a coach and athlete, husband and wife team setting and achieving goals for themselves - and facilitating countless others to reach theirs.

Decades of timeless and selfless dedication are a trademark of their passion for sport, and each other. I found their wonderful relationship tangible, their frankness refreshing and their professionalism....well unquestionable.

They are and continue to be the 'Remarkable Kyles'